ITALIAN AUTHORS
OF TODAY

PETER MICHAEL RICCIO

ITALIAN AUTHORS OF TODAY

Essay Index Reprint Series

BOOKS FOR LIBRARIES PRESS
FREEPORT, NEW YORK

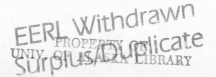

First Published 1938
Reprinted 1970

INTERNATIONAL STANDARD BOOK NUMBER:
0-8369-1842-8

LIBRARY OF CONGRESS CATALOG CARD NUMBER:
75-128298

PRINTED IN THE UNITED STATES OF AMERICA

TABLE OF CONTENTS

TO THE READER

It is not our intention to present here either an exhaustive or an authoritative study of contemporary Italian literature. The proximity of the time element and the complexity of the recent and current literary tendencies in Italy render such a task difficult if not impossible. Realizing the dearth of texts in English on contemporary Italian letters, we have been content to try to indicate a few trends, and more particularly to record personal reminiscences of certain writers.

After a long, tedious experience of compiling notes on critical estimates of Italian authors, the thought finally dawned upon us, one day, that what we were doing was merely recording a conglomeration of other people's impressions that made little, if any, impression on us. We determined therefore to cease getting information through second and third hand sources and to go out and study the creators of literature in their own native atmosphere. So we prepared bag and baggage and took a boat for Naples. In this study, therefore, we have naturally stressed those authors whom we have been privileged to know during our recent literary peregrinations through Italy.

We take this opportunity to express our sincere thanks to the Council on Research in the Humanities for material assistance rendered in the preparation of this volume.

P.M.R.

INTRODUCTION

Years ago the literary salon used to serve as the haven or meeting place for men of letters interested in discussing the literary topics of the day or desirous of organizing a new school of literary thought. In recent years in Italy the cafés have become more and more the centers of the important cultural and intellectual skirmishes.

In Rome we found the headquarters of the traditional forces of the literary élite in the Caffè Aragno. There at one of the tables the poet Cardarelli, considered by some the generalissimo of the Roman division, expounded his Leopardian theories of style and solicited the aid of such veterans of the pen as Ungaretti, Barilli, Cecchi, Baldini.

In Florence it was Paszkowski or the Caffè delle Giubbe Rosse where the Tuscan *letterati* gathered to wage war upon the "decadent" school of Italian writers. These Florentine cafés share the honor of having been the cradle of some of Italy's most important literary and artistic movements of the last decades. For it was here that the *Voce*, the *Lacerba*, the *Selvaggio* and the *Solaria* groups were formed to carry on their cultural and literary operations.

The *Voce,* directed by Giuseppe Prezzolini, was one of the most important reviews published in Italy during the ten years preceding the World War. Among its more active collaborators were men like Croce, Gentile, Papini, Soffici, Amendola, Salvemini, Boine, Slataper, De Robertis, Jahier, Cecchi, Lombardo-Radice and Serra. These men sought inspiration not from without but from within their own artistic souls. They wished to see through their own eyes and not through the eyes of others. They exercised no little influence in giving new life and vigor to the subsequent trend of Italian literature.

Two of the finest essayists of the *Voce* Group, Renato Serra and Scipio Slataper, died heroic deaths on the battlefield, soon after the outbreak of the Great War. Italians today revere their memory not only as great soldiers but also as great men-of-letters. In Serra's *Esame di coscienza di un letterato* and Slataper's *Mio Carso* may be detected the spiritual creed of the new generation in Italy — a creed which stresses self-sacrifice and heroic living as necessary antecedents to a worthwhile life.

The literary activity of the *Voce*[1] was interrupted by the World War and no literary review of importance was to appear until 1919 when *La Ronda* was founded in Rome by Vincenzo Cardarelli. His chief collaborators were Emilio Cecchi, Riccardo Bacchelli, Bruno Barilli, Antonio Baldini and Lorenzo Montano. The *Ronda*

---

[1]For detailed discussion of Prezzolini and the Voce movement consult *On the Threshold of Fascism* by the author.

group, tired of the violent extremist reactions of Futurism, aspired to a return to Italian tradition-al forms and sought inspiration from the writings of Leopardi and Foscolo. But the artificiality of a movement which had its start in the imitation of others was soon apparent and *La Ronda* ceased publication after a few years. It did, however, serve to encourage a little more care and discipline in Italian literary forms.

In Florence, directly across the street from Paszkowski, which was the rendezvous of many of the *Voce* writers, is the Caffè delle Giubbe Rosse. Here the newest and the youngest of the Florentine school of writers met for its daily pow-wows. We often enjoyed the privilege of sitting at the same table with such budding authors as Arturo Loria, Raffaello Franchi, Alberto Carocci, Giansiro Ferrata, A. Bonsanti, and, last but not least, Eugenio Montale. It was indeed a treat to study the daily routine of this group of writers who met every day at noon at their favorite café. The order of an *americano rosso* or of an *espresso* was merely a material point of departure for the spiritual and intellectual program that was to fol-low. The agenda of the day often included indiv-idual reports of the reading done during the morn-ing hours or since the cenacle of the night before. Sometimes it was a new book to be raked over the coals, occasionally it was a remark made by some "stupid" writer in the literary column of the morning newspapers. (Italian newspapers have for years daily devoted their third page to a dis-cussion of books and authors). And not infre-quently the order of business called for a consi-

13

deration of the activities of the older literary group across the street at Paszkowski's or of the Roman crowd at the Aragno. And here it might be interesting to note that on occasion the boundary limits of discussion sometimes extended to authors beyond the Alps and across the Channel to England. Yes, sometimes it even spanned the Atlantic to America. For these young writers were still thick in the fight between *strapaese* and *stracittà*. They believed that a thorough apprenticeship in letters could best be served by not being confined to the narrow limits of one's native literature.

Feeling very keenly what they considered to be the current decadent manifestations in literature and in art, this young Florentine group of the Giubbe Rosse established in 1926 a monthly review called *Solaria* whose title was to be symbolic, perhaps, of the need for a new and invigorating atmosphere to shake off the lethargy and intellectual stupor of the times. One of the primary functions of *Solaria* was to help solve the problem of the younger Italian writer who had difficulty in placing his article or his manuscript with a publisher. Italian publishers, like all others, do not care to gamble with writers who still have a reputation to make.

Unlike so many of its literary predecessors, *Solaria* pretended to have no really definite or fixed program of activity. Too many reviews with a stipulated program of literary propaganda had sooner or later disintegrated or succumbed to material as well as intellectual exhaustion. Yet it was this very lack of a definite program that caused *Solaria* to cease publication recently.

The first issue of *Solaria* appeared in January 1926. Among the early contributors were Alberto Carocci, Raffaello Franchi, Bonaventura Tecchi, Arturo Loria, Piero Gadda, G. De Benedetti, A. Bonsanti and Eugenio Montale. The early numbers do not reveal an exclusive interest in literature for we find articles dealing with artists like Felice Carena, Baccio M. Bacci and G. Colacicchi. The more interesting issues of the first years are the *Numeri Unici*. One was devoted to the writings of Italo Svevo whose *Coscienza di Zeno* is considered one of the most im portant psyhcological novels published in Italy. Another was devoted to the works of Umberto Saba, one of Italy's representative contemporary poets.

It may be interesting to note that practically all of the *Solaria* group are what the Italians call *autodidatti* or self-taught. Franchi is the only one who has gone through a university. The materialistic side of life has little appeal for them. To attain financial independence through a successful career in medicine, law, business or politics is of secondary consideration. And yet, with one or two exceptions, none of them can ever hope to derive a livelihood out of their literary endeavors —at least for some years to come. The royalties over a period of two years from such a favorably received book as *Il Cieco e La Bellona* would not be sufficient to provide the author with more than a month's living expenses in Florence. To live by the pen in Italy today is still as difficult as it was years ago.

It is indeed inspiring and illuminating to those of us who worry over financial reverses to be able to mingle with these young writers and to observe how little it takes in a monetary way to supply their daily needs for food and shelter. A number of them rely upon little odd jobs here and there for material sustenance. A few monthly articles in Italian newspapers help pay the rent. Those who cannot find a market for their literary wares either trust to Providence or are generally taken care of by their more fortunate and successful colleagues. If the morning's mail brings in a check for back pay on manuscripts published, it often is a signal for general jollification at the noon reunion. A banquet is very likely to be announced for that very evening to which the whole "gang" is invited. Then the lucky author, unable to restrain the sudden flush of opulence, proceeds to Seebers in Via Tornabuoni to purchase some of the latest books by favorite native or foreign authors. When, however, funds are low and there has been no pay for some time, this same writer may be seen walking the streets of Florence with perhaps the very same books under his arm looking for some second-hand dealer who will take them for enough cash to bridge over the current economic crisis. Yes, these literary customers of the cafés of Italy may feel the lack of cash and material comfort like few writers in other countries where the economic stringency is much less felt, but we question whether these latter lead a life any more enlightened, or any more spiritually

16

intoxicating and exciting than the table lizards of the Aragno of Rome or the Giubbe Rosse of Florence.

Many Italian writers of the recent decades in their attempts to unshackle the heavy chains of tradition that seemed to impede their forward march and in their desire to give expression to the new social and intellectual order set up by modern developments have, however, gone to extremes in their efforts to repudiate the past. Their eagerness to overthrow the old order has made them renounce the good as well as the evil in the work of their predecessors. As a result many have developed a distorted or unbalanced sense of esthetic values. They smile on their ability to say nothing. And they have nothing to say. Yet, they say it so well.

Today in Italy, and for that matter in other countries too, there are many young writers whose works reflect a minimum of historical and literary background. The fact that these young men possess scanty knowledge of or little appreciation for the great authors of the past is a tremendous handicap to them. Somehow, one cannot help but express surprise at the number of contemporary novels that have very little significance and that are almost totally lacking in artistic intuition or expression. A few personal reminiscences of one's adolescence interspersed with the consideration of one's sex problems have too often been the excuse for writing a novel. Freudian theories have infiltrated the literary cafés of Italy and the vogue has led not a few to entertain the notion that in the phenomenon of sex, with its attendant social complexities, is to be found the only source of literary inspiration for the writer of today.

Of all the authors who have expressed a predilection for a discussion of the phenomena of sex in the social structure of modern life, the only writers to enjoy a relatively moderate success have been Antonio Moravia with the publication of *Gl'Indifferenti* and Luigi Bartolini with his *Passeggiata colla ragazza*. But both these books have won popular favor in Italy more because of their attractive literary style than because of their content. There were many books we read, however, that seemed to be built on the flimsiest of structures. They offered nothing in the way of style or representation and they had little, if anything, in the way of sentiment, emotion, lyricism. If, as the new artistic criticism teaches us, the classic school of writers stands for *rappresentazione* while the romantic school stands for the expression of *sentimento*, then most of these modern authors possess neither of these two elements. And according to Croce, both are indispensable for the production of a real work of art. If, to stand the test of time, a modern novel, poem or painting must contain the characteristics of both the classical and romantic schools, then, with but very few exceptions, all the authors and publications of modern Italy as well as of Europe and America seem doomed to ephemeral fame.

As for the current trend in Italian poetic compositions, E. Falqui and A. Capasso published in

1933 an anthology entitled *Fiore della lirica italiana dalle origini ad oggi* in which they set forth their ideas concerning the essential character of Italian poetry. According to these young men, that which gives particular tone to Italian verse is its *lirica pura*. But even a superficial acquaintance with the works of the present-day poets would fail to substantiate their theory concerning the *"poetica estetica"*. Present-day poets in Italy reveal too bewildering a diversity of theory and subject matter.

The Futurist movement, sponsored by the irrepressible Filippo T. Marinetti and his group, represented a violent reaction to traditional standards and more especially to the poetic forms of Carducci, D'Annunzio and Pascoli. But the reaction was too violent and extreme for the tenacious traditions of Italian literary tastes. Hence the Futurist movement had a rather short life in Italy and left much less of an imprint there than elsewhere on the continent. It did, however, serve to reveal the need for a renovation of Italian poetry.

A noteworthy attempt to instill new life into Italian verse and to get away from the theories of Carducci, D'Annunzio and Pascoli was made by the "Twilight Poets" or *poeti crepuscolari,* as the critic G. A. Borgese first called them. Tired of singing lofty themes, in lofty meters, these Twilight Poets, somewhat after the manner of the French verse of Rimbaud, Laforgue and Verlaine, began to sing of ordinary things, of trivial things in a melancholy mood.

Guido Gozzano was the recognized leader of the Twilight School of Poets. The other members were Sergio Corazzini, perhaps the most attractive of the group, Fausto Maria Martini, Corrado Govoni, Marino Moretti and Aldo Palazzeschi. Gozzano, Corazzini and Martini are now dead, the first two, victims of tuberculosis at an early age.

The titles of some of the works of these poets reveal their attraction to the trivial or every-day things of life. For example one of Marino Moretti's volumes is entitled *Poesie scritte col lapis,* another is entitled *Poesie di tutti i giorni.*

Rather than the sunrise, these poets prefer to look at the twilight. Their favorite themes are the evening, marking the death of day; Sunday, which marks the end of the week; Autumn, with its attendant fading and withering, marking the coming of the end of the year. The poetic images and emotions are not often clear, perhaps, to symbolize the shadows and dim light of the evening. Their melancholia is often saturated with irony. It is not derived from the conviction that life is unbearable but rather from the belief that man is not the all-important being he thinks he is, that he really plays an insignificant role in the world about him. Hence it is not surprising to find that they are often amused at themselves. Palazzeschi for instance in his often-quoted poem *E lasciatemi divertire* says:—

> After all, I am absolutely right,
> times have changed a great deal,
> men no longer ask anything of poets:
> so, let me have a good time!

Present day critics in Italy have naturally relegated the Twilight Poets to a past generation. The post-War poets who have supplanted them manifest different ideals. There is much less uniformity among them. Of the post-War poets one who has attracted a good deal of favorable criticism is Eugenio Montale whom we discuss at length elsewhere in this volume. But Montale's fame rests on only one volume *Ossi di Seppia* (Turin: Gobetti 1925).

In the poems of Giuseppe Ungaretti and Aldo Capasso, there has been detected a link with the French poet, Valéry. Ungaretti is the author of *Allegria di Naufragi*. In 1923 there appeared a reprint of the poems of this volume, with some additions and a preface by Mussolini. When in 1931 Ungaretti published *Allegria*, the title itself, along with the preface, indicated a new optimistic trend in literary creations and in Italian mentality in general. Ungaretti's world is quite different from that of Montale. Ungaretti writes of *tormenti formali*. A perusal of his works seems to indicate that he is primarily occupied with form. Some one has compared his compositions to Chinese miniature poems, with an appeal more to the eye than to the mind. Here is an example:

"Soldati."

Si sta
come d'autunno
sugli alberi
le foglie.

21

"Soldiers,"

Standing
as in autumn
on the trees
the leaves.

Ungaretti's facile style was bound to attract
imitators and among the most important we
might mention Salvatore Quasimodo, author of
Oboe Sommerso (Genoa: Edizione di Circoli,
1932); and G. Titta Rosa, author of *Feste delle
Stagioni* (Florence: Solaria 1928).

An interesting feature of the work of certain
contemporary poets is the apparent link with the
phenomenon of Fascism. A desire to react against
the fruitless melancholia and fragility of the Twilight Poets and to reflect at the same time a more
optimistic mental note is evidenced in the work
of Vincenzo Cardarelli who has a virile, vigorous
style and puts a good deal of emphasis on the
arte di tacere. In contrast with Ungaretti, Cardarelli does not believe in *lirica pura,* in reducing
"words to pure sound". Cardarelli wants body
and vigor in his verse. He does not depend solely
upon rhythm and sound. Another poet who expresses a return to traditional form and also attempts to give body and vigor to his verse is the
young Florentine, Berto Ricci. His work reveals
unmistakable traces of Carduccian influence. Even
more strongly Fascist in tone than Ricci, perhaps,
is the work of Carlo Betocchi. Indicative of this
is the title of his *La Realtà vince il Sogno* (Florence: Il Frontespizio 1933).

Among the poets who possess a genuine philosophical background is Umberto Saba, native of Trieste. He has written some of the finest verse of the recent decades. There is something reminiscent of Shelley in his *Preludio e Fughe* (Florence: Solaria 1928) which contains strong musical and philosophical undertones.

The only Italian publication devoted entirely to contemporary Italian verse is *Circoli*. It was founded by Adriano Grande, a poet of autobiographical themes and of *crepuscolari* echoes. *Circoli* has printed the original verse of such poets as Sergio Solmi, Barile, Pavolini. Of more interest to American readers, perhaps, is the fact that *Circoli* not long ago devoted an entire issue to translations of American verse forms. It contained an interesting introduction by Prampolini, and advocated a rapprochement between American poetic experiments as typified by the "Active Anthology" and the Italian experiments in the field of *lirica pura*. *Circoli* represents one of the more interesting of the recent phases of Italian contemporary verse but its keynote is one of pessimism and hence directly opposed to the youthful and hopeful spirit of the present régime in Italy.

I.

THE INFLUENCE OF DE SANCTIS

Without doubt, one of the outstanding contributions made to the cause of modern learning and scholarship has been the great impetus given in recent years by Italian scholars to a richer and more enlightened appreciation of what constitutes literary and artistic activity. The purely naturalistic and positivistic concept of literary criticism is out-of-date in contemporary Italy. Today there is a marked tendency to avoid the pitfalls of scholars who, after years spent in the accumulation of mere facts and inexhaustive data, generally produced meaningless and stultifying academic publications that manifested little if any insight into the fundamental spiritual problems involved. And the pioneers in this movement for a more enlightened appreciation of artistic values have been such Italian thinkers as De Sanctis, Croce, and Gentile.

Important, however, as is the contribution of these Italian writers to modern thought, their influence is only now beginning to assert itself in European intellectual circles. In America few indeed are the discriminating critics whose knowledge of De Sanctis and Croce go beyond the mere recognition of their names; and this is the situation in spite of the worthy and persistent propaganda of Americans like Arthur Livingston and J. E. Spingarn, the latter of whom, it is interesting to note, dedicates his excellent book entitled "Creative Criticism" to "Benedetto Croce, the most original of all modern thinkers on Art."

With the Romantic Movement there developed in Europe a tendency to free more and more criticism from the old traditional conception of the Greeks and the Romans, whose main canon for the appraisal of a work of art was whether or not it was true to nature. Even in the 19th century there were those who still considered art as secondary to civil and religious activity, as a sort of ornamentation, as it were.

The French had been more or less agreed that criticism was expression, Mme. de Stael believing that literature was "an expression of society"; Sainte-Beuve, that it was an expression of personality; Taine, that it was the expression of race, age, and environment; but the Germans were the first to give a more exact philosophic interpretation of criticism and to convey the idea that art had performed its function when it had expressed *itself*.

Carlyle, observing developments in Germany wrote: "Criticism has assumed a new form in Germany. It proceeds on other principles and proposes to itself a higher aim. The main question is not now a question concerning the qualities of diction, the coherence of metaphors, the fitness of sentiments, the general logical truth in a work

26

of art, as it was some half century ago among most critics; neither is it a question mainly of a psychological sort to be answered by discovering and delineating the peculiar nature of the poet from his poetry, as is usual with the best of our own critics at present; but it is, not indeed exclusively but inclusively, of its two other questions, properly and ultimately a question of the essence and peculiar life of poetry itself. The problem is not now to determine by what mechanism Addison composed sentences and struck out similitudes, but by what mechanism Shakespeare organized his dramas and gave life and individuality to his Ariel and his Hamlet. Wherein lies that life, how have they attained that shape and individuality?''

While the Germans expounded the new doctrine, they did not always successfully apply it in practice. When, about 1840, Francesco De Sanctis read Hegel, the latter revealed to him a new world of critical thought. Especially interested did he become in Hegel's notion of art as having an autonomous function. But this concept although affirmed by Romanticism was never clearly defined. Hegel himself was very hazy on the subject. He treated the history of humanity as the realization of ideas, art being the progressive effort towards the attainment of an idea. Once the idea was realized, art disappeared. Art thus acquired a real spiritual value but even here it seemed to assume a secondary position.

De Sanctis, who had a greater intuitive sense of art than Hegel, soon began to feel the insufficiency of this concept. While for Hegel art was spiritual insofar as it represented an idea, for De

Sanctis form was an expression which had an absolute value in itself. All that was not realized in this form; i. e., a form that had an absolute value in itself, was not art. De Sanctis tried to see an artistic form persistent in itself. Then followed the great effort to separate form and ideal and to apply it in the world of art. For De Sanctis form became idea, and it was to be pure form or expression and not a mere reflection or an ulterior ideality.

De Sanctis accepted the triple Hegelian partition of art into symbolic, classical, romantic; but he believed it could be explained by a principle independent of Hegel's idea. "This principle is the great problem of the universe: God, man and nature, enigmas to which the mind turns constantly." [1]

In De Sanctis there is always the fundamental thought of the ideality of art, of art as an expression or form of the ideal. He proceeds to the reconstruction of the antecedents of a work through a study of the fundamental problems of a given author's times and philosophical, moral and religious *credo;* in this manner he can penetrate the genuine significance of a work of art. These antecedents are essential to the understanding of a work of art and without them a critical estimate is bound to dwindle into meaningless formalism.

De Sanctis may be found to share the Hegelian thesis of art as the incarnation or form of the

---

[1] See De Sanctis, F., *Teoria e storia della letteratura*, Bari, Laterza, 1926, Vol. II, pp. 106-107.

ideal except that De Sanctis is more determined to safeguard its separateness. He declares that "the ideal is only content, and that content is the raw material, the *datum* of a problem — for the real issue is the following: given this or that content, does it live? However new, interesting, or abstract the content, it has no value if the poet has not the power to elaborate in his own mind and reproduce it as something new and throbbing. Now this interior process and resultant creation in scientific language is called *form*. It is not, however, to be confused with the misleading connotations of the term, form, as commonly used by rhetoricians."

In form is the essence of art. De Sanctis in his *Saggio critico sul Petrarca* says, "If in the vestibule of art you wish a statue, put form into it . . . the esthetic appears when there appears form, in which that world is immersed, fused, forgotten, lost."

Art, like all great human activities, has its roots in the ideal: the work of art is not a fact, nor a physical thing, but it is always a human ideal, since to be human means not to be satisfied with fact, but to go beyond the facts, to seek out their significance, their interpretation.

Man seeks the ideal in the fact, in physical reality, and as a result we have science. He has a knowledge of his supreme ends, and he wants to realize them; hence his moral ideal. The exigencies of order and harmony arouse the desire to produce a world in which the idea and the matter are perfectly incarnated and as a result there arises art. He is an artist therefore who is capable of moulding, adapting or arranging the sensual world of colors, lines, sounds, according to the aims of his ideal, aims which life only imperfectly realizes. Art therefore is a synthesis of ideal and form. [2]

It is commonly believed that to appreciate a work of art all that is necessary is to place it before oneself, so that it alone may speak to us and tell us what it is—in the same manner as one may see a picture with one's eyes or appreciate a piece of music with one's ears—and that this is the best if not the only manner to do so; i. e., to make an abstraction of every human reality, to shut oneself up in the world of the images of the artist just as, in order to dream, one must drive away every image of consciousness.

But with this premise one runs the risk of merely scratching the surface of a work of art rather than appreciating it; a work of art considered as an image shows only its nude outward form whereas one must penetrate within and discover the revealing kernel, the first germ that motivates it to the ideality of the artist, to the world of his beliefs and convictions.

---

[2] The following quotation from De Sanctis' essay on Parini may serve to clarify his idea on art:

"Senti dire: l'arte per l'arte: massima vera o falsa secondo che la s'intende. Che a fare l'opera d'arte si richiede l'artista, vero. E che scopo dell'arte sia l'arte verissimo. L'uccello canta per cantare, ottimamente. Ma l'uccello cantando esprime tutto sè, i suoi istinti, i suoi bisogni, la sua natura. Anche l'uomo cantando esprime tutto sè. Non gli basta esser artista deve esser uomo. Cosa esprime se il suo mondo interiore è povero, o artefatto, o meccanico, se non ci ha fede."

We only fool ourselves by considering art as pure image, for when the ideality of the artist is simple and of common possession, we are likely to believe, owing to the ease with which we understand or perceive it, that there is nothing to it except the pure image. Indeed art is not mere form but an ideal which is realized as form. And since it is necessary to penetrate the ideal of the artist, who as an artist is a man, and as such belongs to a certain epoch, possessed of certain ideals, aspirations, tendencies, one may see clearly that esthetic criticism to be complete, must take into consideration the psychological and historical factors. The appreciation of a work of art comes about when it is traced to its very source, to its generating centre: to the soul of the artist who is necessarily a man of a certain century with certain ideas and ideals. And he is that much greater as an artist, the more vast is the ideal to which he has given form, the wider his knowledge of the progressive aspirations of humanity. This does not mean that one should examine each work of art to determine what is true or false, good or bad, but that the significance of a work of art is inseparable from the comprehension of the human ideal and that the greater or lesser amplification of it differentiates the impeccable fragmentary lyric from the vast cosmic construction like the Homeric, the Dantean and the Shakesperian.

De Sanctis had a better knowledge of European literature than of classical literature but profound indeed was his knowledge of Italian literature; and in his critical estimates of Italian letters there is one constant and important aim running throughout: the proper understanding of artistic values.

The purely biographical and bibliographical conception of literary history does not interest De Sanctis. It is not the usual chronological compilation of authors, of dates, of events, of literary movements. Literature for De Sanctis is primarily the expression of the human spirit in an inseparable relation with its moral, social and political history. De Sanctis' "History of Italian Literature" is fundamentally a history of the Italian people, beginning with the thirteenth century and continuing down to his times. Each writer's work is considered in its entirety. The contributing moral, political and economic factors current in an author's life are neither neglected nor given disproportionate treatment.

The critic, according to De Sanctis, must not place before himself abstract rules and subtle classifications and proceed to judge the *Divine Comedy* with the same criteria with which he might judge the *Iliad* or the *Orlando Furioso*. The critic's duty is to study the world the poet has created for himself. He must examine it, inquire into its nature, analyze the organic laws, the concepts, the style and manner in which it has been brought forth. He must know how to sift extraneous matter. It wasn't the political ideal behind Dante's poetry that determined its ultimate value. Shelley had different political notions from Dante. And while Shelley was imbued with notions of democracy, Shakespeare had strong leanings toward aristocracy. Yet they were all great poets. Whether the political ideal of the one or the other was good or bad is beside the point. What mattered was the poetic expression of their ideal.

De Sanctis possessed that rare, artistically intuitive attitude of mind, so essential to the intimate appraisal and enjoyment of a work of art, in a degree which no literary critic has exhibited before or since his time. He knew how to discover the true inwardness of artistic beauty; he was singularly skilled in identifying and plucking the petals of its elusive flower. De Sanctis entertains and instructs the reader not by exalting and admiring authors but by interpreting them in the light of his own rich and extensive human experience. As an interpreter he reveals an uncanny skill in separating the dead from the living elements of a literary work, in making us feel its artistic unity through the unity of his criticism.

De Sanctis' remarkable critical instinct is illustrated in his appraisal of *Dante's Inferno*:

. . . ."*Hell* is the Kingdom of evil, the death of the soul, the empire of the flesh, choas; esthetically it is ugly. Some say that the ugly is not a subject of art, for art is the representation of the beautiful. But all that is alive is art, and there is nothing in nature that may not be art. Like nature, art generates and its creatures are not individuals, not species or genera, not *types* or specimens, they are *res*, not *species rerum.*"

Of *Purgatory*, he says "he who wishes to understand Purgatory should place himself in that age of life when passions have grown less violent, when with experience and disillusionment the personal and active elements have diminished; man feels himself in the mood for generalizations;

he finds he belongs to a class . . . He is now a spectator rather than an actor, and life manifests itself not as an active force but as an artistic, philosophical and religious contemplation. The passions appear before the soul but they are no longer its passions; they are outside, contemplated in others, with the eye of a penitent man. Passions, good and bad, are not present and in action but they are a vision of the spirit, represented in images. Here then you have the world of waiting, of serenity, crowned by the artists: Casella, Sordello, Guido Guinicelli, Arnaldo Daniello, etc. Dante, not as a mere spectator but as an actor, sets forth the new concepts and the forms of the spirit world, freed from flesh or sense."

Art gives body and life to this world; it gives it form, but observed in the purity of the kingdom of the spirit how could it be represented? Dante humanized it by making it accessible to the senses and the imagination; he made it the expression of a new civilization, a world of sentiment and imagination throbbing with personality, lighting up the impersonalism of the Middle Ages with the glow of glory and setting the stage for modern letters.

In De Sanctis, along with a great feeling for art, there is always a great sureness of critical method. What is more, he knows how to criticize without debasing. He knows how to incite and correct without discouraging. There is almost always an affection for the author he treats. He understands full well that there is no poet who does not have his days of feeble inspiration, of distraction, of weakness.

De Sanctis is convinced that a poet does not say nor can he always say all about himself. The critic must bend every effort to fill in the rest, to complete the picture, by joining in a spiritual unity with the poet. The poet, according to De Sanctis, "is an harmonious echo that repeats only a few syllables of a word; but an echo animated and endowed with a conscience, which feels and sees more than is revealed by its sound. The critic gathers these few syllables and guesses the entire word. He distinguishes the steps and the gradations; he seizes the intermediate and accessory ideas; finds the sentiments from which the action springs. the thought that qualifies it, and the throb-generating image; he projects his glance into the inward and invisible parts of that world of which the poet has only given you the corporeal veil."

Through the drama of literary history we behold in De Sanctis' writings the panorama of Italian civilization unfolding itself before our very eyes. The pages of his *History of Italian Literature* are so stimulating, entertaining and enlightening that they read like a novel. They seem to have a development and continuity of interest that are rare indeed in the annals of literary criticism.[3] It is not surprising, then, to find Brunetière stating that "there is no work that is better or more philosophic, or more agreeable to read."

---

[3] Only recently has De Sanctis been rendered into English. The beautiful American edition of De Sanctis, translated by Joan Redfern, in two volumes, with an introduction by Benedetto Croce, will satisfy a long-felt want.

It is the common acknowledgement of thinkers and critics, even of opposite views, that the fundamental merit of De Sanctis is to have produced an original criticism based on the concept of the autonomy of art, a criticism that is founded on a demonstration of fact rather than on purely philosophical abstractions.

Outstanding thinkers of diverse and various leanings who occupy themselves with this problem have come to accept De Sanctis' fundamental concept of the autonomy of art, though they may differ in the interpretation and application of this concept.

II.

BENEDETTO CROCE

The greatest living exponent of the thought of Francesco De Sanctis is Benedetto Croce.

Where De Sanctis left off in his critical studies, Benedetto Croce resumed and proceeded to carry the ideas of his teacher still farther. But while De Sanctis expressed a superior critical intuition in his writings he did not display the superior philosophical background of his disciple, Benedetto Croce. Not only does Croce reaffirm the concept of art as autonomous but he traces back the ideas of De Sanctis to their Italian origin, Giambattista Vico. He shows that, aside from certain classifications, there was in Vico a philosophical concept in which art is the first activity of man. Art is the first manifestation of the spirit. Only later when art is criticized does philosophy enter. Art for Croce becomes pure intuition.

Before we go more into detail concerning the definition of art as pure intuition however, let us sketch briefly the early life and activity of Benedetto Croce, whom discerning scholars consider the greatest living exponent of thought and learning in Europe.

Croce, as a young man, grew up in rather

favorable economic and cultural surroundings. His father was a well—to—do landowner whose main concern was the administration of his estate. His mother was a highly cultured woman who encouraged her son's passion for books. He attended the "collegio," a form of boarding school, where he developed a great fondness for history. After the terrible earthquake of Casamicciola, where both his parents and his sister were killed, he spent some years living in Rome with his uncle Silvio Spaventa, the statesman and brother of Bertrando Spaventa, the philosopher. At this time Croce through his uncle came to know the vicissitudes and corruption of political life. He acquired an early contempt for the raucous hollowness of liberal politicians, stupid in unscrupulousness and pompous rhetoric. The greatest experience perhaps of Croce's university life at Rome was his contact with the personality of Antonio Labriola, whose lessons on moral philosphy revived in him a new faith and hope in life. "I felt the obscure danger of materialistic theories, whether sensistic or associationistic. About them I entertained no illusions at all, as I clearly perceived in them the substantial negation of morality itself, in the form of a more or less disguised egotism . Herbart's ethics taught by Labriola restored in my mind the majesty of the ideal, of *that which is to be* as opposed *to that which is*—a mysterious inscrutable opposition, and because of its very mystery, absolute and uncompromising. Those lessons came unexpectedly to meet my harrowing need of rebuilding for myself in a rational form, a faith in life and its aims and duties." [4]

After a few years stay in Rome he went to live in Naples, which has been his permanent and favorite domicile ever since. With the money that he inherited from his father he purchased, for sentimental reasons, the house in which Giambattista Vico had lived, and the shadow and influence of that great philosopher has ever been present in the life and work of Croce.

One of the most significant events in the history of culture of the present century in Italy was the publication in 1902 of Croce's *Aesthetics*. At that time Benedetto Croce had hardly passed his thirty-fifth birthday, but already he had made some very interesting historical studies and had written a treatise on *La storia ridotta sotto il concetto generale dell'arte,* which contained the germ of his philosophy. He also wrote articles in literary journals like the *Fanfulla della domenica* and in *Flegrea* in which, during the years 1899 to 1901, he published for the first time a portion of his *L'estetica.*

Having developed in the midst of the cultural crisis of his day, Croce studied the problem from its very sources and attempted to establish a new equilibrium which should take into account the new forces—*soggettivismo* and *intuizionismo* and the Italian traditions of Vico, Spaventa, and De Sanctis. What motivated the publication of *La critica* in 1903 was the belief—as expressed

---

[4]Croce: *Contributo alla critica di me stesso,* Naples, 1918, pp. 21 22.

later by Croce himself in his review—that one of the greatest achievements performed in the last years in Italy had been the increased discipline, thanks to the universities and other institutions of learning, in the method of research and documentation; and Croce considered himself an exponent of what was called the historical or philological method—*metodo storico o metodo filologico*. But Croce maintained with every bit as much conviction that "such a method is not sufficient to all the exigencies of thought. It is necessary also to promote a general revival of the philosophical spirit so as to enable criticism, history, and philosophy to profit by a conscious return to the traditions of thought which had been unfortunately interrupted after the fulfillment of the Italian Revolution . . ."

Upon the launching of *La critica* he gave as his program for the new review the desire that "it should not yield any quarter to those many genial persons who, oblivious of the history of ideas and of facts, boldly take upon themselves the task of solving the arduous problems which man has attempted for centuries to unravel, secure in the belief that they can be solved by a quick stroke of their would-be prepossessing methods."

The youth of Italy, however, were not prepared to follow the course prescribed by Croce. The painstaking, serious study of their country's past in the field of art and ideas, as a necessary prerequisite for the solution of prevailing ills, was a task that held but scant appeal to a generation wallowing in the miasma of materialism and self-seeking individualism. It seemed as if the zest and enthusiasm that brought about the political unity of Italy, had spent itself in the attainment of that one goal. Intellectually, the country had reached a dead end. There was need of much intellectual prodding before the country could be aroused from its lethargy.

A few individuals there were, such as the contributors to reviews like *Il Leonardo, La voce, Il regno,* who did earnestly endeavor, albeit not always effectually, to spread the quickening message proclaimed by Croce and Gentile. To Prezzolini and his collaborators of *La voce* belongs, in no small degree, the credit for freeing the nation from the deadening grip of intellectual inertia.

In his definition of Art, Croce denies four important considerations. First he denies that Art is a physical phenomenon. It is not the paper on which a poem is printed nor the kind of marble which a sculptor carves that determines the artistic quality of the poem or sculpture. Second, he denies that art is an utilitarian act. To drink a glass of cold water on a hot day may be useful and pleasant but one would hardly say that to do so is a work of art. The figure represented in a painting may evoke the most pleasant memories and the most beautiful associations yet the picture artistically may be ugly. Vice versa a painting that may appear ugly and repulsive to our emotions may possess great artistic beauty. Thirdly, Croce denies that Art has anything to do with morals. Art is something outside the field of morality. Certainly the artistic value of a beautifully carved chair of the Renaissance cannot be determined on moral grounds. Does the fact that a sculptor tells lies, fails to keep his word, has illicit relations with a woman, alter the beauty of a statue he has produced? Lastly, Croce denies that Art has anything to do with metaphysical or conceptual knowledge. Reality or non-reality have no bearing on the esthetic appraisal of a scene. Historically and metaphysically untrue, the image expressed may yet contain the highest form of artistic expression.

Now if art is intuition, expression, vision, symbol, of what, says Croce, is it the symbol or expression?[5] Is it a chaotic accumulation of images? No, intuition is really artistic *only when* it has a vital force which has the power of making all the elements of the intention harmonize irresistibly with it. Croce makes his point clear by contrasting the ideas of the Romantic and Classical Schools of thought.

Romanticism makes of art a violent and spontaneous effusion of loves, of hates, of passions, of despair, of exultation. It is often expressed in vaporous, indefinite images, in broken style, in approximate phrases, whereas Classicism was an effort to seek the placated soul, the symmetrical line, the calm figure, exact in contour, well balanced, clear. If classicism leaned heavily on *Representation*. Romanticism leaned heavily on the

---

[5] "Certo, l'arte è simbolo, tutto simbolo, cioè *tutta significante;* ma simbolo di che? Significante che cosa? La intuizione è veramente artistica, è veramente intuizione e non caotico ammasso di immagine, *solo quando ha un principio vitale che l'animi,* facendo tutt'uno con lei."

side of *Sentiment*. And for many years there have been bitter debates between exponents of the two schools. Of what earthly good is art, say the Romanticists, if it is rich in clear, limpid images and does not speak to the heart? And if it speaks to the heart what difference does it make if the images or the expressions are not so clear or definite? But, answer the Classicists, the indiscriminate piling up of effusive emotional outpourings does not enhance the beauty of an image. On the contrary they mar the picture, distort it. Of what good are all those emotions which one may experience outside the realm of art, if they jar our esthetic taste?

Croce concludes by saying that a true work of art is neither Classic nor Romantic. It is both. For the sentiment without the image is as blind as the image without the sentiment is empty. "L'arte è una sintesi a priori estetica. Il sentimento senza l'immagine è cieco, e l'immagine senza sentimento è vuota." Consider for a moment the real masterpieces of painting, sculpture, literature and what do you find? They not only satisfy the dictates of the Romantic School but they also adhere to the fundamental aim of the Classicists. They have representation and sentiment combined.

According to Croce[6] there are three kinds of literary criticism. First, there is the criticism that takes the form of a pedagogical tyranny that orders and prohibits, approving and disapproving.

---

[6] Croce: *Breviario di estetica*, Bari, Laterza, 1925, pp. 84-90.

It is the kind of criticism before which artists and writers stand in awe or in adulation, inwardly detesting both critics and their criticism. They expect favors which that type of criticism is unable to give and they dread the damages which it is unable to inflict, since it is evident that a critic cannot make an artist out of one who is not, nor can he destroy or belittle an artist who is an artist.

Secondly there is that type of criticism which is concerned with separating the ugly from the beautiful, departing from the principle that there may be in art both the beautiful and the ugly. It assumes the role of a judge attributing to itself the office, not of promoting or guiding the life of art, which is promoted and guided only by history, that is, by the complex movement of the spirit in its historical course, but of distinguishing in the art that has already been produced, the beautiful from the ugly, consecrating the beautiful and reproaching the ugly with the solemnity of austere and conscientious pronouncements. And of what good are these sentences when the judgment has already been pronounced by the genius and the taste of the artist himself. And how often has the judgment of criticism arrived only too late, to consecrate forms already acclaimed or to condemn ugliness already convicted. Such criticism only kills what is already dead and attempts to bring to life what has already been living.

Thirdly, there is the criticism which interprets or comments, explains the linguistic forms, the historical allusions, the antecedents and ideas of a poem and permits the work of art to operate spontaneously in the soul of the observer or reader, who will then judge according to what his intimate taste will tell him to judge. Such criticism serves the useful purpose of a cultured cicerone or a discreet school teacher, but one must be wary of their prejudices, likes, dislikes, habits, omissions, etc.

Now true criticism, in the view of Croce, is not any one of these three but it is all three together. Croce does not deny the possibility of using the results of one of these operations for the purposes of another, but this does not change the nature of either. "The spirit of man is not divided into small compartments: all our experience helps us in whatever work we are doing. To understand Petrarch's poetry, it is useful either to be or to have been in love but it does not follow that to make love and to understand that poetry are one and the same thing."

The critic should ask himself these questions: What have I read? What is the value of that which I have read? What is the genesis and outcome of this particular work? And having answered the three questions, is there one answer that furnishes the key to true criticism? Croce answers this question by saying that it is all three together, for they represent the conditions or better, the antecedents, of criticism.[7] They give a

---

[7] Croce in this connection writes: "E come la critica d'arte ci è apparsa inscindibile dalle altre critiche, così anche la storia dell'arte solamente per ragioni di letterario rilievo si potrà scindere dalla storia complessiva della civiltà umana, entro la quale essa certamente segue la sua legge propria che è l'arte, ma dalla quale riceve il movimento storico, che è dello spirito

reproduction of the image; they are the elements that reconstitute the artist's creation, the artist's expression. They reestablish the condition of the producing artist. But with this, however, we do not reproduce the work of the artist in a new form. We merely give it a translation, a variation. Or as Croce says, "all these three things are the necessary conditions, without which it (true criticism) would not arise. Without the moment of art (and art against art, is, in a certain sense, as has been seen, that criticism which affirms itself productive and a helper or a curber of certain forms or productive to the advantage of others), the material on which to perform would be lacking. Without taste (criticism or judgment) there would be lacking to the critic the experience of art, art that has developed within his spirit, separated from non-art and enjoyed as against the latter. And lastly this experience would be lacking without the exegesis or without removing the obstacles from the reproductive imagination furnishing the spirit with these antecedents of historical consciousness of which it has need and that serve as the kindling with which to light the fire of imagination."[8]

If we are to accept even summarily Croce's theory of art as expression and bear in mind the elimination of the 1. physical 2. utilitarian 3. metaphysical 4. moral considerations, then we

tutto e non mai di una forma dello spirito, avulsa dalle altri. S'intende che la critica è essa stessa creazione e non può obbedire a schemi fissi e sistemi."

[8] Croce: *Breviario di estetica.*

have necessarily discarded a good deal of the old conceptions concerning literature. And to quote the excellent words of Spingarn:

"We have done with the genres, or literary kinds . . . as the lyric, comedy, tragedy, epic, pastoral, and the like, the classicists made of each of these divisions a fixed norm governed by inviolable laws. The separation of the genres was a consequnece of this law of classicism; comedy should not mingle with tragedy, nor epic with lyric. But no sooner was the law enunciated than it was broken by an artist impatient or ignorant of its restraints, and the critics have been obliged to explain away these violations of their laws, or gradually to change the laws themselves. The lyric, the pastoral, the epic, are abstractions without concrete reality in the world of art. Poets do not really write epics, pastorals, lyrics, however much they may be deceived by these abstractions; they express themselves, and this expression is their only form. There are not only three, or ten, or a hundred literary kinds; there are as many kinds as there are individual poets. To slice up the history of English literature into compartments marked comedy, tragedy, lyric, and the like, is to be guilty of a complete misunderstanding of the meaning of Criticism, and literary history becomes a logical absurdity when its data are not organically related but cut up into sections, and placed in such compartments as these. Only in one sense has any of these terms any profound significance, and that is the use of the word "lyric" to represent the free expressiveness of art. All art is lyrical, the Divine

Comedy, King Lear, Rodin's Thinker, the Parthenon, a Corot Landscape, a Bach fugue, or Isadora Duncan's dancing, as much as the songs of Heine or Shelley.

"Every poet re-expresses the universe in his own way, and every poem is a new and independent expression."

If we accept the Crocean definition of art we must also put into the discard such notions as style, technique, metaphors, similes, since all these exist only on the assumption that style is separate from expression. And this conjures up memories of our college days, when to misplace a few commas in Freshman English or to misspell a word was sufficient to warrant an F on a theme or composition. Croce is not concerned with technique, punctuation, spelling, sentence structure, or any of the other accoutrements of the rhetorician's arsenal; rather is he concerned with intuition, expression, creative power.

The new criticism has also done away with the futile and endless discussion as to what constitutes prose and what constitutes poetry. The debates between friends and enemies of *vers libre* are now relegated to the scrap heap. They have been shown to be so much literary refuse. Just as the artistic merit of a poem is not determined by its rhyme or metre, so the artistic merit of a prose work is not determined by the use of proper punctuation, or any special rhetorical forms. It is the imaginative power expressed by the writer that counts. And it makes little difference whether it be prose or poetry. For that matter a history of a people or a scientific treatise may, because of the artistic intuition of the author, contain more poetry or artistic lyricism than a poem with all the traditional outward forms of rhythm or rhyme but lacking in the one essential requirement, imaginative power. Concerning the distinction between prose and poetry all that one can conclude is that prose contains less rhythm than poetry.

III.

GIOVANNI GENTILE

The name of Gentile is closely linked with that of Croce in the recent revival of serious studies in Italy. According to competent students of their philosophies, both started out by following the road paved by Vico and Hegel, but whereas Croce is said to have extended the limits of Hegelian criticism, Gentile's views are considered to be a return to Hegel.

Gentile was born at Castelvetrano (Trapani) in 1875. He studied at Pisa where he first became known through the publication of a thesis on *Rosmini e Gioberti*. After the university he taught philosophy in the lyceums until 1905, when he was appointed to the royal university at Palermo, to assume the title of professor of the History of Philosophy. From 1914 to 1918 he occupied the chair of philosophy at Pisa and then transferred to Rome where he has become the director of philosophic studies. From 1922 to 1924 he was minister of Public Education, and under his leadership the law of 1923 was enacted for the Reform of the Italian educational system.

Throughout their early life and up until

very recently Gentile and Croce have enjoyed a comradeship and a fellowship in their studies that represent one of the most beautiful and inspiring chapters in the history of modern Italian learning and scholarship. The need for a more conscious and active participation in the search for the touchstone of philosophy brought them closely together. In their early journey through the extensive field of knowledge they found much happiness and inspiration in each other's work. Each has felt the undeniable influence of the other to the point where both Croce and Gentile have been obliged to alter or at least qualify their original esthetic concepts. Croce, the elder of the two, was the first to attract the attention of the discriminating public and Gentile followed in his footsteps.

The friendship and comradeship of these two great scholars was not to last indefinitely however as we shall point out later.

Gentile is noted for having developed a system of actual idealism. It calls itself actual just because it starts from the initial concrete thinking act and proceeds to explain everything else as due to the movement from concrete thinking to abstract thought. For Gentile, everything which is in the mind is present in two ways: a thought that is *being* thought out and a thought that *has been* thought out. The act, the process of thinking is in the present; the fact, the result of thinking is in the past. The actual cannot be factual. With Gentile introspection is always retrospection.

"From the standpoint of knowledge, the world neither grows nor decreases in being; from the standpoint of action it is becoming something more or new. In knowing, man looks backwards on a world not of his own making or which he has ceased to make. In doing, he is looking forward to a world he may create or is creating. For knowledge all is made; for action all is still to be made."[9]

"But," says Gentile, "once we admit, with actual idealism, that the object of knowing is the subject himself looking, so to speak, into his own inwardness, thus realizing himself ever anew by his own creative knowing, since Spirit is the only reality and its reality is its activity, the activity by which he knows is the very activity by which he is ever creating the world, that is, his very own self; and thus every knowing, and Spirit appears as a knowing-doing creative activity."

The relation between the world of ideals and the world of realities, between facts and human aspirations, received serious consideration in the mind of Giovanni Gentile, and we find it manifest in the literary production of the last decades in Italy, as for example in the plays of Pirandello, Rosso di San Secondo, and Chiarelli. "Whatever Gentile's efficacy in other branches of life may have been, he had this effect among the men of letters—to give reality, so to speak, to the unreal by elaborating the truth that we live wholly in the present, and the present as present, is beyond our ken (we do not know it until it is past). Though we never know the present in which we

---

[9] Crespi: *Contemporary Thought in Italy*, New York, Alfred A. Knopf, 1926, p. 152.

live as present, there is nothing in it which we do not know a second later when it is past."

"In Gentile the subject or the Spirit is free, not in the sense of being free to choose between two different objects of volition but in the sense that the subject is, in so far as he realizes himself, in and as the process of his acts;" and as Crespi further points out, "it follows that there will be no room for individual liberty and personality in Gentile's philosophy of politics. The true reality and freedom of the individual is that which he gains by losing himself in his family, in his state, humanity." Hence Gentile, shaping his conception of the state very much after the manner of Hegel, has been given the appellation of the philosopher of Fascism, although it must be admitted that Rocco, Carli and Suckert have contributed their share of ideas in moulding the present thought of the Fascist State.

Gentile shapes his conception of the state very much after the manner of Hegel.[10]

---

[10] In his volume *Che cosa è il fascismo?*, he finds a relation between the work of Fascism and the ideals of Mazzini who saw even in his own day that one of the steps towards a unified Italy, towards the development of an ideal nation, was to combat materialism or individualism. For Gentile, in fact, individualism and materialism, its corollary, were the very defects which it behoved Italians to overcome, in order to really feel the love of country and hence to weld Italy together— "per sentire veramente la patria e fare quindi l'Italia."

Mazzini felt that materialism is unworthy of thinking man. He felt that no man's life was really worth living if it was inspired by materialism, which for Mazzini was synonymous with individualism. Liberalism for Mazzini did not mean liberty of the individual above all else; it did not mean

In 1913 there appeared in the issues of *La voce* the first signs of a rift between the philosophic conceptions of Gentile and those of Croce. In his talk at the fourth Philosophic Congress held in Rome in 1920, Gentile reaffirmed the fundamental differences between the philosophy of Croce and his own. According to Croce art is intuition and not judgment. The subject matter of art is the particular and not the universal. This particular is not an object; it is the subject's own state, the subject's sentiment and spiritual attitude as an immediate fact of knowledge. In all this Gentile is in complete accord with Croce. Furthermore Gentile says, "I observe that the basis of this concept is always the subjectivity of the artistic form of the spirit, which bends or is moulded in judging the thought. And he who says judg-

---

individualistic liberalism which does not recognize the nation as above the individuals, which does not embrace the mission that belongs to the people as a whole, nor the sacrifices to which the single human being is bound. Gentile affirms that Liberty should exist, by all means, but that it should be kept within the limits of the State, limits which the individual cannot transcend. A people is a nation not so much in the fact that it has a history, a common past which is materially and definitely ascertained, but rather in the fact that the people feel their history and appropriate it with a living conscience as a part of one's very personality. Gentile views Fascism as an ideal which stresses the greatness and beauty of sacrifice, the mightiest force for the establishment of a well knit and well ordered state. Conversely, the primary function of the State, is the ever increasing improvement of the individual, as a *sine qua non* of its own progressive rise. To this end the government should be adjusted to operate in a system where the real social, economic, and intellectual forces of the country are truly represented.

ment says synthesis of the subject and predicate: subject which is particular, and predicate which is universal—so that every thought is the universalization of a particular subject, which, in its immediate particularity is not thought out but is sensed—it is seen, but one cannot say what it is. It is felt therefore, but without knowing what it is; nor is there any possibility of reflecting on it."

Gentile's theory is a natural consequence of Croce's, and it is a fact that the points of agreement of the two theories are greater than those of disagreement. These affinities derive from their fundamentally similar idealistic conception of art, affinities which are, without doubt, the result of the reciprocal influences they have exercised upon each other.

In Croce there is more of the historian. In Gentile there is more of the philosopher. For

---

But what is even more significant is that Fascism, according to this philosopher, wishes to attack in the most intransigent way the "myths" and the "lies" of socialism, "the exploiter of the sentiment of justice and therefore of individualism in the name of an abstract and empty ideal of human brotherhood." Rather than delude the working men with delightful dreams and highsounding words of an ideal socialistic state working for their interests, Fascism conceives of a realistic state functioning not in words but in actual facts for the betterment of the workingman and his family. That is why Fascism has as its constant aim the organization of a state morally bound to the welfare and future of the working class. It proceeds from the consideration that the national government should not be the harbour or refuge of professional politicians who purport to represent the will of the people. The government should be adjusted to operate in a system where the real social, economic, and intellectual forces of the country are actually represented.

Croce philosophy is really criticism and method-
ology. For Gentile philosophy is the heir and
substitute for religion, and he is interested in conclusions rather than in the method. With Croce
there is a tendency towards distinctions, whereas
with Gentile there is a burning craving for unity.

Now it is undeniable that the concept of art
as creation is asserted time and again by De Sanctis
and that it is set forth as the equivalent of the
concept of autonomy. Art is neither history, nor
morals, nor science, declares De Sanctis; it is creation, that is, absolute independence. However,
aside from the fact that the obscure concept of
creation does not necessarily imply independence
of one form from another but only a relative
independence; since independence from other
forms still implies relationship.[11]

Gentile endeavors to conciliate the opposing
views by considering the life of the spirit as a
synthesis of dialectical moments. If the spirit is
divided into radically different faculties it would
be difficult to explain their relation and the passage of the one to the other. Instead the passage
between two ideas becomes clear if they are considered as forms of thought that from the first
passes to the second, just as a man is first a child
and then an adult, so that the two ideas continue
and yet maintain a reciprocal and dynamic difference.[12]

[11] Albeggiani, Ferdinando, *L'autonomia dell'arte in Francesco De Sanctis e nell'estetica italiana contemporanea*, Roma,
Associazione del mezzo giorno, 1932.

[12] Gentile: *Sommario di pedagogia generale*, Bari, Laterza, 1914, Vol. II, p. 8.

Gentile's doctrine assigns to art a function necessary in the life of the real, defines clearly its relation with other manifestations of the spirit, renders intelligible the passage from one manifestation to another; but it does not appear to justify the autonomy of esthetic criticism, or the separateness of individual works, a cardinal point in the thought of De Sanctis.

Gentile's doctrine leads to the conclusion that pure and distinct works of art do not exist; that is to say, works that, although including all the values of the spirit, are presented under the exclusive form of art; and this consequence De Sanctis would certainly have refused as destructive of his critical method. De Sanctis distinguished between works of science and works of art whereas, in Gentile's theory, the distinction is not permitted between the artist and the non artist; i.e., between Dante and Galileo, but only between artist and artist, beween Dante and Fazio degli Uberti.[13] Is it possible in Gentile to maintain the value of the fundamental distinctions in the common judgment and critical estimate and speak of a history of art that is not a history of science, a history of science that is not a history of philosophy, a history of philosophy that is not a history of mathematics?

At present the distinction is not at all clear. For if the criterion of evaluating cannot be but one; i. e., philosophical, the scientist will declare that the dominance of the soul over the concept is an error, but art will refuse to receive such a

---

[13] Gentile: *Filosofia dell'arte*, p. 220.

baptism and declare to the scientist that it is not concerned with questions of reality.

Without underestimating the value of Croce's contribution to the study of esthetics, his admirers recognize the existence of several obscure points. Albeggiani observes, not without reason, that the application of Croce's criticism to the concrete individualization of a work of art often leaves us dissatisfied if not unconvinced. It does not take sufficiently into account the ideality of art, an extremely important consideration in De Sanctis. Gentile[14] in a very recent article entitled *Torniamo a De Sanctis*, although not mentioning his illustrious colleague by name, undoubtedly had him in mind when he stated "a great many of his (De Sanctis') ideas are found in other writers, perchance even more clearly expressed; but these writers remain a thousand miles distant from the 'truth' of De Sanctis." [15]

There is no doubt that Croce himself has felt certain gaps in his esthetic doctrine, since he has seen fit to alter and modify his early notions

---

[14]In Quadrivio, August 6, 1933.

[15] And Gentile adds:

"It is high time to tear away the cobwebs of that unattainable criticism which seeks in vain to divide the indivisible, to fix an ideal moment in the life of the spirit: art, fine art, poetry as opposed to prose, form conceived apart from content etc. If art could be pointed out as something apart standing wholly by itself, it would be revealed to be but an absurd refuge for man. But whenever man has experienced a genuine form of art, he has invariably felt in it the pulsation of his whole humanity, with all its faith and pasiin; nor can any man ever set himself apart from humanity, without falling headlong into an abyss of false living and false art.

of art, in which he first defined art as a knowledge of the individual, then later as pure image, as lyricism, as expression of the sentiment, as a stage of the spirit, as a moment in the circle of the life of the spirit, as reflecting all in its form. Step by step he has reached the thesis propounded in his essay *Il carattere di totalità dell'esperienza artistica,* [16] which is nearest perhaps to the concept of De Sanctis. But Croce has always given art an auroral character which is difficult to conciliate with the complexity of a work or art. [17]

The crux of the problem then is to give absolute value to esthetic activity in such a way that it must always be found in the spirit; and it is impossible to conceive of a spirit that is devoid of it. The relation of this activity to the others must be shown in a manner that it is itself and at the same time in relation with others.

What constitutes the distinctive character of both Croce's and Gentile's doctrines is the consideration of art, or better of the activity of the spirit that generates art, as a first and necessary

None the less this does not mean the abandonment of form and the return to content. It means the abandonment of false form for true form, of the artists' art for the art of living men, of learned poetry and literature for the poetry of the human soul, the only authentic poetry.

[16] See Croce's *Nuovi saggi di estetica,* Bari, Laterza, 1920.

[17] Albeggiani on this point adds that *auroralità* can only mean the ideal antecedence of feeling over the consciousness of feeling. This reflection of feeling in assuming as its object the many-hued world of images, will apply to them the qualification of reality and unreality. And there is no doubt

step or moment in the life of the spirit; as a necessary first step, because without it the life of the spirit would be impossible, whether it is called science, religion, philosophy or mere experience. It is *a necessary chronological and logical* step in Croce, who in this way approaches closer to Vico and to human experience; but only logical in Gentile, who in his search for unity derives his concept from the Aristotelian form, or better from the transcendental Kantian form, which is distinguishable only logically and not chronologically from the fact of experience.

In both doctrines there is an attempt to consider art as an absolute reality from the standpoint of the spirit.

Both doctrines are *not* satisfied with the simple statement "art exists;" they are not content to point out its particulars. They wish to show what is art; and why, granting the existence of the spirit, art must inevitably exist, just as Descartes from the existence of his *ego*, inevitably infers the existence of the world.

Croce in fact says you cannot deny that the spirit exists. And no matter how you might wish

---

but that reflected thought acts thus as regards poetry, for Plato criticises the unreality and the immorality of the Homeric fables, and Saint Augustine condemns poetic drolleries. And for this reason we moderns condemn as illegitimate such criticism which instead should appear legitimate in view of the auroral conception of art which considers art as an antecedent of scientific thought in so far as material for scientific elaboration. With scientific elaboration we imply the right of science to treat art as matter and hence the right of the scientist to invade the realm of art to ask—are you true or false?

to consider the spirit as perception, will, etc., here it is before you as art, for the universal presupposes the individual; that is, art (Croce's first form of esthetics) or the knowledge of the real must have as a basis the real as feeling (second form). Or as Gentile says, the knowledge of the world, of the object, if the spirit is absolute reality, is also knowledge of the subject.

In both, then, fundamental is the attempt to justify art or to demonstrate it by connecting it to the life of the spirit as a subordinate element, as a moment or step which is found again in the superior moments or steps, just as the seed is found again in the plant or the infant in the man.

But in spite of the apparent superiority of De Sanctis' critical intuition over both Croce and Gentile, to insist too much on what some have considered the few points of obscurity in their critical structure, would be like failing to see the forest for the trees. Taken as a whole there can be no denying the tremendous import of the work of Croce and Gentile, in the development of a more enlightened literary and artistic criticism. De Sanctis, Croce and Gentile are an inspiring triumvirate in the search for a more enlightened scholarship and learning. And concerning specifically the contributions of Croce and Gentile to contemporary thought we have found no better summing up than the following words of Crespi:

"Through the instrumentality of Croce and Gentile, through their examples even more than through the ever-increasing volume of their work, a new generation has been, and is still being, trained in literary, historical and philosophical thinking, which by means of this very thinking is becoming more and more aware that neither individuals nor nations are mere tools of cosmic, economic or human necessities, . . . that, through making nature and history the objects of our thinking, we break their spell, we make them ours, we rise above them and begin life anew. In this feeling of restored initiative and freedom, in this opening of new horizons to the Italian mind, in this revelation of a possible new mission for Italy and Italian culture, of a mission of deliverance both from materialism and from supernaturalism and ecclesiasticism, and of faith in the divinity of man, more than in their systematic philosophies, is to be sought the key to the great success of Croce and Gentile in making their countrymen — and not them alone — so conspicuously their debtors.''

IV.

OTHER CRITICS

While the academic and university circles were at first rebellious or at least diffident to the new Criticism, the fact remains that today the influence of Croce is being more and more felt wherever there is any semblance of artistic and literary activity. Not only institutions but publications, reviews, newspapers are beginning to express a more living and conscious interest in artistic problems. Instead of the traditional dilettante anecdotes and pleasanteries of the old school of journalists (Panzacchi, Nencioni, Scarfoglio) there is now diffused in Italian journalism a new tone of seriousness and severity that borders on the scientific.

What was lost in the way of petty but precise details has now been made up by a readily recognizable pathos. During the first decades of the present century, Italian scholars and for that matter European scholars as well were displaying an arid and narrow spirit of erudition. Art and literature were often the objects of a scientific and historical research that was almost totally divorced from the living and palpitating substance that composed the works studied. On the other hand it is only fair to acknowledge that this type of academic pedantry was impregnated with a good deal of intellectual honesty and sincerity.

There were, on occasions, instances of a real though naive appreciation of letters and poetry. Italian scholars like Pio Rajna, I. Del Lungo, Comparetti and D'Ancona had given rise to a whole flock of erudite and academic investigators: Novati, Rossi, Flamini, Mazzoni, Cian, Scherillo, Crescini, Bertoldi. One almost saw traces of the eloquence and taste of Carducci who stood between the intuitive, romantic tendency of De Sanctis and the erudite, historical, academic school. In D'Ovidio and Cesareo there was a faint shadow of De Sanctian influence but they felt too strongly the attachment to the historical and positivistic conception of Criticism.

One of the more useful and positive aspects of the academic critics was to be found in the new editions of the classics (the Biblioteca Scolastica, the Giusti collection of Livorno, the Barbera of Florence and the Vallardi of Milan). But even here the main preoccupation seemed to be exactness of dates, facts, with too much space devoted to ridiculous pedantries and aberrations. In recompense however, there was always a profound love and respect for the author studied. In all it was a heap of useful, serious and conscientious work to which many, tired of the futile and nebulous esthetic disquisitions and dialectical exercises of many *pseudo-crociani,* turn today with grateful acknowledgement as if anchored on sure and safe ground. On the other hand one should not overlook the fact that their work appears like so many noble efforts of by-gone days, wrought with old-fashioned notions, with tools and implements that are now out of date.

Among those on whom the influence of Croce was not profound but who managed to write critical studies of note, special mention should be made of F. Torraca, E. G. Parodi and A. Farinelli. In the work of Torraca one can detect a sprinkling of De Sanctian tradition attenuated and deviated under the influence of the dominating individuality of Carducci but also enriched and supported by a solid and extensive historical and philological background. Torraca has gained much recognition for his excellent comments on Dante.

Parodi even more than Torraca fell under the influence of the historical school. In fact, he was one of its most ardent exponents. In the preface of a late publication he said he "wished to be boring and solid rather than brilliant and superficial." Parodi has written some interesting essays on Dante, correcting the judgment of De Sanctis on a number of episodes in the "Divine Comedy." He also published a worthy study of Iacopone.

Arturo Farinelli has fought for many years against the narrow and restricted attitude of the historical school of literary thought. Few professors are as extensively cultured or possess the knowledge of so many languages and literatures as Farinelli. His writings display an enthusiasm for literary investigation. They cover a wide range of subjects and have obliged him to break the barriers of the historical method and of preestablished classifications. In his best works Farinelli does not confine himself to a discussion of the poetic work but attempts to recreate the psychological personality of the author who produced it. But the person who appears most living and apparent in his writings is Farinelli himself, the dashing and bold knighterrant of modern letters.

With the diffusion of Croce's *Estetica* and its attendant discussions and polemics, there developed, as we have already pointed out, a strong dislike for the erudite and narrow methods of the past. At times this dislike for specialized and technical studies has been exaggerated and unjust. Yet there is no denying the fact that the sincere followers of Croce are expressing a more extensive culture, a more actual and enlightened modernity, richer in problems even extraneous to the world of letters but more actual. Hence academic criticism is now joining hands with journalistic criticism. University professors are writing articles for Italian dailies. They are becoming interested in contemporary Italian and foreign literature. They try to follow the new schools of poetry. Journalists deliver lectures from university chairs and the names most frequently mentioned are Croce and De Sanctis.

Unfortunately not all the studies that purport to bear the stamp of Croce and the new school of criticism contain a well disciplined and ripened analysis. Many express a woeful lack of a solid, organized interior life, guided by laws and purposes, well-defined and clear. There is too often an unmistakably false and superficial tone underlying their work. Many made the initial error in believing that since art is expression, any form of expression is therefore art.

From the defects of the new school, from the aberrations of taste and from the facile and presumptuous tendency towards generalizations and summary judgments, certain men of the academic or university school of thought are saving themselves. In this category we should place men like Bertoni, who has written some excellent essays on Muratori, Ariosto, and the early period of Italian literature; De Lollis, for his study on Tasso; Manacorda for his essay on Foscolo; Trabalza for his research on Boccaccio; Casella for his book on Iacopone; and others like Toffanin, Neri, Ezio Levi, Salza, Scarano. Even more successful than these latter are the critical writings of Trompeo, Praz, Zottoli, Petrini.

Of the younger men who have received the baptism of Croce's *Esthetics* and who have remained more or less true to the faith of their spiritual father, special mention should be made of Luigi Russo. Russo is better fitted to treat critical questions than he is to discuss the literary work itself. His *Narratori* is a series of short excellent essays on the prose writers. Russo has also published interesting studies on Metastasio, Verga and Di Giacomo.

Renato Serra who is now dead was one of the most esteemed and beloved of Italian critics. In Serra there was always a conscious desire for clarity and unity. Serra tried to diagnose modern restlessness and decadence in a very sincere and convincing manner. His studies on Panzini, Beltramelli and Pascoli are masterpieces of critical analysis while his book *Le lettere* is indispensable for an enlightened understanding of contemporary Italian literature.

Donadoni, like Serra, died a premature death. He too possessed a strong personality that is reflected in his books and even in his style, simple, sober, clear. In his studies Donadoni reconstructs and analyzes the complicated psychological processes by which poetry originates in great authors. His essays reflect a keenness of artistic appreciation whether they deal with the life or with the thought of the writer. He has published a very good study on Foscolo. His book on Tasso is even more esteemed.

Types like Slataper, Boine, Gobetti, all of whom are now no longer living, have left excellent examples of critical studies that express an almost immediate recognition of what is false and what is true in artistic intuitions.

Momigliano in his criticisms is always seeking the expression of a lofty idea, a broad humanity, an intimate life, and not an exterior harmony. He is quicker than Donadoni at grasping the esthetic values of a work of art and knows how to reveal the most secret beauties. His writings touch all periods of Italian literature but his best contributions are his interpretations of Ariosto, Poliziano, and Manzoni.

Giuseppe Borgese, who is at present teaching in America, possesses a marked capacity to reconstruct the psychological make-up of a writer. A cultured professor and a brilliant lecturer, Borgese is considered among the best of Italian literary critics. He is the author of a number of important volumes and of one of the most discussed and representative novels published since the World War. In this novel, *Rubè*, Borgese gives an excellent picture of disillusioned youth returning from the war seeking renewed faith and hope in religion.

Borgese first attracted attention in the days of the *Leonardo*, the review founded by Papini in 1903. It was in this review that he published his article on *Metodo storico e critica estetica*. The article elicited the praise of a number of discriminating readers and won for him the plaudits of Benedetto Croce.

His university dissertation on the "History of Romantic Criticism" *(Storia della Critica Romantica)* is still considered a classic of literary studies.

For many years Borgese was the literary critic of *Il Corriere della Sera* in whose columns he reviewed the most important books of the day. Not infrequently he brought to light a young budding author whose work was worthy of merit. He had the uncanny and happy faculty of picking out and introducing to the public those books which sooner or later were to become the daily topic of conversation in literary circles. The most recent examples of this rare critical intuition were his presentations of Moravia's *Gli Indifferenti* and Cinelli's *Castiglion che Dio sol sa.*

Borgese has often befriended the young writer and has a large following among the younger generation of authors and readers. He has lectured in foreign countries where his originality of interpretation, his eloquent delivery and his extensive culture have made him much esteemed as a critic and a scholar.

Emilio Cecchi is another critic whose name has become familiar to readers of *Il Corriere della Sera* and whose critical works have won much esteem because of the delicacy and originality of their workmanship. But of Cecchi we deal at length elsewhere in this volume.

Another critic whose name appears often in Italian periodicals is Adriano Tilgher. Tilgher with philosophical leanings of his own has tried to outline a system of esthetics in opposition to that of Croce. The results however of this attempt have been scanty. Tilgher in his studies attempts to evaluate not so much the intrinsic value of the literary work of an author but the culture and civilization from which the work originates, and the ideals and moral tendencies that it expresses. He is so sincere in his critical attitude that he often succeeds in penetrating not only the substance of a literary production but the soul of the author himself.

A writer who has broken away in recent years from his youthful theories is Giuseppe De Robertis. Equipped with a rich cultural background he has developed an appreciation and a vision of art that is not only less abstract but more human. His studies on Leopardi have received much favorable comment. Together with Pietro Pancrazi, De Robertis directed the literary criticism of the short-lived attractive literary review: *Pagaso,* Both De Robertis and Pancrazi express a keenness and refinement of artistic taste that is the envy of many of the younger critics of contemporary Italian letters.

One who has tried unsuccessfully to detach himself from Croce is Alfredo Gargiulo. Gargiulo first attracted attention as a critic by his very interesting study on D'Annunzio. In this book he gave evidence of possessing a subtle and detailed appreciation of what constituted real artistic expression in literary productions. In his later studies, however, Gargiulo suffers from a tendency to exaggerate the depth and the minuteness of his literary approach to the point that he appears at times to be indulging in a monotonous, tortuous, and involved game. Gargiulo contributed some stimulating articles on contemporary authors in *L'Italia letteraria*, the recent literary weekly of Rome. In them he is very favorably disposed towards the work of the young poets and especially Montale in whom he visualizes the desperation of the present generation of youth without ideals, battling the sterility and acidity of modern civilization.

Of the younger critics who have made a favorable impression upon the literary salons of present day Italy and who express the influence of Croce in their work, those especially worthy of mention are Francesco Flora for his volume on *Dal romanticismo al futurismo* and Camillo Pellizzi for his excellent study on *Lettere italiane del nostro secolo*.

Others who have contributed noteworthy critical studies are Sapegno, Piccolo, Lipparini, Ravegnani, A. Consiglio, De Benedetti, B. Migliore, Angioletti, Franchi, Caiumi, Soloni, Vinciguerra, Commisso and Palazzi. The best critical analyses of the theatre have been given by D'Amico, Praga, Simoni, Bacchelli.

Of the anti-Crociani the most outstanding critic is Galletti. But even Galletti reflects a cultural desire and an intellectual curiosity without the old tradition of limits. Galletti suffers perhaps from an excessive facility to describe vast phenomena in too rapid synthesis.

Summarizing the effects of the new school of literary thought we may say that Croce's conception of criticism has contributed materially to a revival of Italian studies that will eventually represent one of the really important and permanent achievements of these decades. It has elevated scholarship and learning to a level never before touched since the time of De Sanctis. Today there is a revival of learning and a desire to reevaluate the past that has not existed for many years. Serious books are being read and critical interpretations are being made of them. There is a love of scholarship and learning not experienced in the last forty years. When a follower of Croce attacks a problem in research today, he first considers all the available sources and facts, he discards the unimportant, then he finds the relation of the important factors upon life, upon aesthetics, and he concludes by giving an evaluation and interpretation of his findings and signalizes those points which throw added light upon our aesthetic conceptions of life, and indicates their relative contribution to the spiritual enrichment of our human existence.

As a result of the work of De Sanctis, Croce

and Gentile, Italian literary criticism today has no restrictions or specialties. All that is art, thought, or history may become a problem of the mind, a subject for criticism with a view to reconstructing and rethinking the artistic universe. Contemporary criticism now goes beyond the naturalistic, sensualistic, moralistic psychological aesthetics. It represents the first important effort to clarify the lyrical and universal character of artistic intuition and the anti-sociological conception of the history of art.

V.

PIRANDELLO, NOBEL PRIZE WINNER

One might readily conclude from reading Pirandello that his primary object is to make us understand that we really do not understand each other. It appears that the motivating force in all the plays of this indefatigable writer is the ever-recurring problem of reality. And the questions that almost invariably suggest themselves to the reader are: What is real in life and what is illusion? What is the personality of this character? Who is he? Who is she? Who are they? And soon the reader finds himself wondering: And who am I?

The goal to which the "theatre of the mirror" aspires is to objectivate dramatically the profound transformation that takes place in the soul of a man when the situation in which he has been living for years, without his being conscious of it, is suddenly revealed to him in all its shameless and terrible nakedness. and he sees himself finally *for himself* the way others had seen him without his knowing it, and what the others imagined he was *to himself* . . . a lightning transformation from the blind and unconscious life to the knowledge of life, from *being* to the *consciousness of being*.

In the words of Pirandello, "When one lives,

one lives but does not see oneself living. But supposing one sees himself in a mirror, a prey to one's passions: either one remains astonished or bewildered by one's very aspect or one turns away in order not to see, or disdainful, one spits upon the image, or mad, one hurls one's fist against the mirror to send it crashing to the floor; and if one were weeping, he can weep no longer, and if he were laughing, he can no longer laugh, etc. In short, a problem obviously arises by force. This problem is my theatre."

In *Tutto per Bene* for example, we see the protagonist Martino Lori, a widower for over sixteen years, absorbed in the amorous cult of his deceased wife. His daughter Palma has been brought up under the care and tutelage of his intimate friend and protector Senator Manfroni; and it is Manfroni, rather than Lori, who selects a husband for Palma. Palma had received so much attention and so many favors from Manfroni that Lori is more regretful than surprised when she shows more understanding and affection towards her benefactor than towards him. But one day, through a word that escapes the lips of Palma, the world in which Lori was living suddenly crumbles from under his feet and he appears to himself as we imagined he had been. Manfroni had been the lover of Lori's wife and is the father of Palma. Manfroni, Palma, and Palma's husband and all their friends had always believed that Lori knew it and merely hid his shame in order to make his job and career more secure through the influential protection of Senator Manfroni.

Lori realizes for the first time that his blindness was so colossal as to render impossible the belief that he had been acting in good faith, and that his friends, now that he sees it clearly, had always treated him with scorn. Yet he could not blame them if he had not been able to see through it all. They certainly did nothing to hide the truth from him.

The mirror through which he sees himself reflected makes him visualize very clearly the terrible wretch he has been for years in the eyes of everyone. He turns away in horror and nausea. But Palma comes to console him and she, her husband, and Manfroni now in turn come to realize that he really never knew, and even for them a new situation is created. Lori is worthy, therefore, of pity and esteem. What is to be done? There is no way out except to continue at least in public, the old comedy. It is the only escape, and perhaps "all for the best" or *Tutto per Bene*.

Although fascinated by the task of uncovering the bare, often crude, realities of life, Pirandello does not admonish us to cease being hypocrites as Chiarelli seems to in *La Maschera e il Volto*, but rather exhorts us to assume more intelligent, philosophic and tolerant attitudes toward society. After all, is not today's tragedy tomorrow's comedy, today's reality tomorrow's illusion?

"Guai se non vi tenete più forte a ciò che vi par vero oggi, a ciò che vi parrà vero domani, anche se sia l'opposto di ciò che vi pareva vero ieri." (Enrico IV, p. 111)

This duality between the real and one's idea of the real enables Pirandello to view the moving drama of existence from an infinite number of viewpoints, to reveal us to ourselves and to each other as clever actors with masks ready for any exigency. Pirandello has no message in the ordinary sense of the word. He does not deal in morals or ethics. He considers man not as a sociological phenomenon but as an irremediable creature to be studied with the delicate instrument of pessimistic humor.

As for our masks he appears to regard them as necessary expedients. Speaking through Liolà, he says:

"Fingere è virtù e chi non sa fingere non sa regnare." Liolà, p. 32.

And in Enrico IV, p. 69

"Guai a chi non sa portare la sua maschera sia da Re, sia da Papa."

It is natural that the keen and intrepid manner in which Pirandello presents the problem of illusion and reality makes for some rather amusing and humorous situations. And Pirandello has always maintained that fundamentally he is a humorist. In Pirandello true humor arises when a man begins to take stock of his own consciousness and begins to think of his existence. Man does not merely live his life, but also thinks it. Hence he becomes both spectator and actor. This is what distinguishes him from the rest of nature.

Plants and animals exist but man not only exists but thinks and has ideas about his existence. And while the process of life moves on incessantly and changes constantly, the mind of man does not always keep pace with life itself, so that man's mental images of himself and of his existence do not always conform with the images of himself reflected in the world outside.

In his drama, Pirandello seems to delight in turning the whole situation topsy-turvy on both sides of the footlights and even outside of the theatre, as he did when "Six Characters in Search of an Author" was presented for the first time, and provoked among critics and spectators a battle as bitter as that which broke out after the famous production of Hugo's *Hernani*. Complacent, peace-loving spirits, smug in their conception of the soul as homogeneous, complete, coherent, refused to be routed and driven from their strongholds, comfortable and pleasant, even though made of cardboard. Equally indifferent to plaudits or censure, Pirandello remained unperturbed by the demonstration.

In "Six Characters in Search of an Author" he sets a tragic drama inside a sheer comedy and presents the contrast between the reality of a character in itself and the appearance of reality with which the actor invests it. The stage director in the play is at first annoyed, then he becomes incredulous and plays a delightfully comic role representing admirably the average man who seems to have more faith in masks than in the truth.

It is perhaps natural that Pirandello's passion for the theory of multiple personality should lead him to the consideration of lunacy as a dramatic element. However, in at least two of his plays, *Enrico IV* and *Il Beretto a Sonagli*, the leading character merely simulates madness. Enrico IV who has regained his sanity, continues to feign lunacy and amuses himself by having his truths taken for ravings. He constructs his universe of dreams and forces the world to adapt itself to his dreams. And when he commits a murder, he buries his crime under the mask of the lunatic. Thus he plays a trick on those servile followers who see him to bed with medieval lanterns and then turn on the electric lights for themselves.

It would be interesting to trace in the works of Pirandello the German influence to which he was subjected as a student in the University of Bonn. At that time the vogue for pathology and the study of mental diseases was popular in Western Europe, particularly in the University centres. Pirandello may not have accepted all the new theories but certain it is that his works reflect this influence and there can be little doubt that he owes to Germany many of the tendencies that moulded the specific form in which his humor is cast.

Pirandello is so eminently capable of combining tragedy and comedy that this faculty alone would establish his claim to the title of humorist in the generally accepted sense of the term. Nowhere is this better illustrated than in *Il fu Mattia Pascal,* his best known and most successful novel.

The protagonist, son of a well-to-do landowner, loses his wealth and is inveigled into marriage with a slovenly, irritable wife whose Xantippe of a mother transforms the house into an inferno. Pascal, suddenly finding himself in possession of an unexpected sum of money, decides on a temporary release from torture and in the course of his journey arrives at Monte Carlo where he is favored by an unprecedented stroke of good fortune. Returning home with his new-found riches he reads in a newspaper the news of his own death. A decomposed body, recognized as being that of Mattia Pascal, has been found in the mill-pond and buried with due ceremony. Dead, is he? Well, that is another stroke of good luck. Following Destiny's cue, he assumes a new name, a new mask, and attempts to lead a new life. This, however, he finds impossible. One cannot live outside of life. He cannot even buy a dog to cheer his lonely hours for that would mean registration and a possible investigation into his past.

In the end, realizing that: "Fuori della legge, e fuori da quelle particolarità liete o tristi che sieno, per cui noi siamo noi . . . non è possibile vivere . . ." (Mattia Pascal p. 292), he throws off his self-made mask, assumes the old one composed by circumstances and returns to his wife. But in the meantime what has happened? He learns that his wife has remarried. What is there to do? Nothing remains but to take up his old duties of custodian (rat-catcher, he facetiously terms his position) in the ancient library where we leave him writing his memoirs.

Not a very cheerful theme! Yet Pirandello has managed to invest the whole story with a redeeming humor that dispels the inherent gloom. Indeed, it is one of the most remarkable novels of modern European fiction. Even in his most desolate moments, when he peers through the mirror of life and sees the clear case of his own desperation, Pascal shows a sense of humor. It seems to glint in Pirandello's own eyes. For many of the facts and circumstances of *Il fu Mattia Pascal* may be paralleled in Pirandello's own life and the author may have puppetized himself in the hero.

Pirandello's versatile genius manifests itself most completely in such novels as *Il fu Mattia Pascal*, and in his short stories, where probably as the result of complex experiences he is now bitter, now gay, now sombre, now buffoon. Indeed, when depicting country life, Pirandello's humor has a spontaneity that contrasts advantageously with his pessimistic reflections on middle-class life. And in his portraits of middle-class life there is a vigor, a credulity, a passion, a realism that makes Pirandello rise above all the short story writers of contemporary Italy, if not of Europe. Indeed, it is not difficult to detect a strong moral undertone in Pirandello, although it is often hidden to the casual reader who does not see beyond the plot itself.

English readers of Pirandello's works are accustomed to think of him as a dramatist but Italians have always considered him primarily a short story writer. As a matter of fact, Pirandello's plays have not had in Italy anything like the success they have enjoyed in other countries, whereas his short stories have been generally acclaimed by Italian critics. And the reason is not difficult to find: Italians are by disposition an intensely realistic people. Hence they are reluctant to accept the Pirandellian dramatic thesis that we know not what is real. The dualism of form and reality or the theory of multiple personality represents the passage from the state of naturalism to that of imaginative caprice.

Then what may be the serious shortcomings in the works of Pirandello?

In the first place to claim that because men at times misunderstand realities they can never really understand each other is an exaggeration, to say the least. If men cannot understand each other, of what use is there to speak to them? Of what use is there to write? To propound the theory of multiple personality is ultimately to deny personality. It may be true that, given certain circumstances or situations, he same individual will reveal a different identity or personality, yet there seems to be a constant that makes it possible for us to distinguish George's personality from that of Henry. The course of a river may change or veer sharply at certain points, yet it seems ridiculous to deny that that river has no general course or direction.

Most of the characters in Pirandello's plays are of the extreme or mentally unbalanced types. They startle our imagination more than they win our heart. There is a flagrant lack of great human sentiment. There seems to be little if any poetic feeling. They seem especially fitted for creating dramatic effect more than for stirring the human soul.

Perhaps there has been too much haste in judging Luigi Pirandello either one way or the other and who knows whether those who have severely criticized him are as much at fault as those who have been most ready to applaud his every word. After all, most people will agree that man's control over his life is very limited.

The past no longer belongs to him. The future is not yet his, while the present is but a "strange interlude." All man can do is to shape the present to suit himself as long as he conforms to the requirements of a constantly changing life.

VI.

GIOVANNI PAPINI

Giovanni Papini, one of the more widely read authors of Italy today, is among the most admired and at the same time among the most criticized. The present century with its changes, its uncertainties, its aspirations, its illusions has no more outstanding representative of the good and bad it has to offer. Already in the early 1900's Papini began to visualize the intellectual instability of modern society, the insufficiency of modern scientific culture, the shallowness of purely philosophical notions of existence. He sought relief from the monotony of life in untiring efforts to satiate an almost unquenchable thirst for knowledge — a *smania di sapere* as he called it.

As a young man Papini read many books, consulted numerous encyclopediae, spending days and nights up in his bare little room, studying, digesting, and copying piles and piles of notes. He soon developed a desire to write an encyclopedia himself. He believed no perfect encyclopedia had yet been written. But before he had gone through the letter A he gave up in despair. Then one day he decided on a more modest undertaking: the writing of a universal history. After working a short time on this subject he saw the utter impossibility of writing a general history of the world, so he made up his mind to write a history of religion. This also became too big a job so he subsequently went down the scale from a history of religion to a comparative history of the world's literature, and from that to a history of the Romance Languages; later abandoning the history of the Romance Languges, he decided on a history of Spanish letters, finally ending up by writing no history at all. This constant effort to carry out vast programs, to attack problems with a hasty and sweeping consideration, is one of the chief characteristics of the early life of Papini.

Papini early became bitter against society for having deprived him of the usual pleasant experiences of childhood. This he attributed partly to his own economic and physical drawbacks, which he says, made many people shun him. Later he began to distinguish clearly the two distinct camps that were being pitched upon the social and intellectual battlefield of his time. The one against which he found himself entrenched contained those who stood for "poetry, literature, elegance, snobbery — in a word — for that D'Annunzian spirit which was beginning about that time to swell the heads and rot the brains of the prematurely senile youth of Italy". It was perhaps about this time that Papini took as his motto for life the line from Petrarch which states, *Io venni sol per isvegliar altrui* (I came only to awaken others).

In his autobiography, *L'Uomo Finito*, Papini describes very graphically how he managed to perform this noble task:

"I came to arouse people, yes; but arouse them not by coaxing them, tickling them, but by using a club on their backs, gripping them by the front of their coats, and slamming them back against a wall that their shame and anger at such insulting treatment might force them to a show of gumption, an act of real manhood. I behaved toward men much as animal trainers go at their lazy sleeping lions in a menagerie. I jabbed them in the ribs, I burned them with hot irons; I gave them ferocious cuts with the whip—jabbed them with the most bitterly sarcastic thrusts I could find; burned them with hard cruel epithets and pitilessly sincere accusations; whipped them with sneers at the meanness of their lives, the insignificance of their ideals, the primitiveness of their ideas, their ignorance of everything, and their incapacity for deep understanding and sound reasoning.

"No one was safe from my sudden and rapid offensives. If there was no question up for discussion I brought one up on purpose, starting an argument on my own territory, involving my opponent in difficulties of my own making and raining merciless blows upon him. If there was a real issue I would turn it and twist it in such a manner that I alone was left on the battlefield brandishing syllogisms and hurling vituperation to the right and left. If some timid individual appeared, I would force him to say something and then I would ridicule him for its absurdity. If I met a garrulous talker I found indescribable delight in humbling his assurance and reducing him to silence. If an unpleasant truth could be told to anybody I was always the first to come out with it without evasion or circumlocution. If I was aware of a defect, a shortcoming, a weakness in any one, I soon found a way to take advantage of it for a pointed thrust or a formal indictment. When my friends wanted to rid themselves of a bore, a timetalker, a pedant, a fool, they left the matter to me; and exceptional indeed the case where he did not disappear once and for all in confusion and humiliation. I had but to find the hidden canker in a man's soul to make it eventually the subject of remark, bluntly accusing him of it *coram populo*. And no sooner had I sensed the most vulnerable and painful point in some person's inner life than I touched on that point and focused attention upon it. A random unguarded phrase and I was capable of drawing the most unexpected conclusions from it, developing its implications, showing its remote bearings on character; and I would hammer and beat upon them until my poor victim begged for mercy or took to his heels. A few spoken words sufficed me to analyze the psychology of almost any man, and when I had taken it to pieces I would put it together again and set it down with a thump in front of him that he might see himself as others saw him and blush for shame." [1]

When Papini is in this destructive mood there are few among the living or dead capable of escaping his wrath. Someone once said that if, on one of his rampages, instead of using a pen he

---

[1] *Papini, Giovanni, The Failure, translated by Virginia Pope. New York. Harcourt Brace & Co., 1924.*

were to wield a pistol, he would leave no person alive and would exterminate even his friends, including Prezzolini, his most intimate one. And it is Prezzolini who tells the story of a Florentine who was known to have once attempted suicide. One day, this Florentine gentleman was introduced to Papini, and Papini upon shaking his hand is said to have remarked:

"Oh, are you the gentleman who once had the golden opportunity to do something really good for yourself and failed?"

But there is another side to Papini. He may be bitter, sharp and outspoken in his reactions to people. He may not mince words. He may speak of ropes in the house of a hanged man. He may be performing the best vaudeville act on the literary stage of Italy, now appearing in the garb of a radical, now in that of a conservative, one moment mimicking an agnostic and the next a believer. Yet those who can read between the lines and especially those who have had the privilege to know him personally must realize that Papini's bark is worse than his bite. His outbursts against society and individuals merely conceal a friendly and sentimental soul. His hatred is there to hide his greater capacity for friendship. He is like an ugly and unappetizing apple which upon being eaten reveals a very sweet taste.

Since the Great War Papini has produced many books and written numerous articles. A bibliography on Papini would entail much labor and cover many many pages. There is hardly a country where he is not known nor a language in which he has not been translated. But what, in substance, is revealed by all of Papini's literary activity?

Throughout Papini's life there has been a constant and uninterrupted restlessness of intellectual craving. We find that he has worshipped on many altars: pragmatism, anti-socialism, futurism, Buddhism, realism, anti-Catholicism and then Catholicism. Is it any wonder that people have often inquired and still inquire: what next?

The intellectual instability of Papini, his repeated changes of idealistic attachments are mostly due, however, to his possessing a lyrical soul that is easily enthused over some new philosophy not yet realized. He fights a philosophy when it does not suit his own personal needs, when it fails to solve the enigma of life, when it fails to provide that peace or tranquillity of soul that is the goal of every modern thinking man. A personal acquaintance with Papini has convinced us that in all his changes of heart he has been sincere. Indeed the most remarkable thing in him is his sincerity. He has not been afraid to confess when others would have been only too anxious to conceal. And why should he be severely blamed if the world itself is so chock-full of paradoxes.

"I repudiate all my utilitarian past. Men want something for all they do. Even such actions as seem prompted of the spirit—acts of love, faith, creation—expect an equivalent return, ask, sooner or later, for payment. Nothing for nothing. Even religions, the arts, the philosophies, all are based on gain. Every human act without exception is a note of exchange which demands cash. The date of maturity varies. Some notes fall due in another life, in heaven, or in ages to come—but the day of reckoning will fall at last. If men were convinced that any part of their labor would be unrecompensed forever they would stop work right where they are. Even God insists upon His reward in prayer and sacrifices. He has reserved a special section in Hell's prison for His bad risks." [2]

But there is no need to resort to the critics of Papini to obtain an appraisal of his life and works. In *L'Uomo Finito* he gives a most vivid picture of his own character, of his own ambitions and failings. In this masterpiece there is no need to concoct a plot, to invent characters, to think up adventures in order to hold the interest of the reader. Here Papini performs the task by the most thorough autopsy ever held over a human mind and soul. No more scathing criticism has ever been heaped upon a well known writer as Papini here heaps upon himself.

"And all my life, even in later years, has been the same—a perpetual reaching out for the whole, for the Universe, only to fall back to Nothing—to a humble seat on the grass behind a garden hedge. My life has been a succession of vast ambitions and hasty renunciations." [3]

"I do not ask for bread, for fame, for pity. I do not ask women for kisses, bankers for money, 'geniuses' for praise. These things I can do with-

---

[2] *Ibid*
[3] *Ibid*

out, or I can steal them, or earn them. What I ask for and plead for humbly on bended knee, with all the fervor and all the passion of my soul is: a little certainty. Something I can believe in with surety, just one, small, tiny atom of unquestionable Truth.

"Rather than die of hunger like an alley cat, I will take up any trade, I will pick rags in the streets with a pack on my back. I will stand in front of churches and restaurants begging pennies in the name of God. I will be a cleaner in a public latrine. I will lead a dancing bear through country towns. If, really, I can find nothing else to do, I will become a lawyer." [4]

Of all the books Papini has written none has aroused so much comment nor met with so much popular success as *La storia di Cristo*, the book that heralded the conversion to the Catholic Church of a writer who had been one of its most out-spoken and bitter critics. But the best of Papini's lyricism is not to be found in *La storia di Cristo*. It is rather in *Pilota cieco*, in the *Tragico quotidiano*, in *Cento pagine di poesia*, and more particularly in his *L'Uomo finito*. In these works Papini writes for the sheer joy of writing, not so much to convince others or to preach to himself but simply to pour out his soul.

There is no comparison between the merits of *L'Uomo finito* and the more popularly acclaimed *Storia di Cristo*. *L'Uomo finito* or "The Failure", as it was rendered in English, is the

---

[4] *Ibid*

lyrical expression of the mental anguish and restlessness that has pervaded twentieth century life.
It is a poem of Liberation and of Victory. It is
really a happy book even though it speaks of
sadness.

Many critics have scoffed at Papini's conversion to the Catholic Church. Some have gone so
far as to say that it is but another of his temporary
attachments. It has been claimed that in the books
published after *La storia di Cristo* Papini expresses
the same old skepticism, the same old change of
"heart". But we are inclined to believe that it is
a little too premature to judge so hastily and so
summarily what may be the most momentous de-
cision Papini has made in his life. In talking
to him and in hearing him express himself we
failed to notice any semblance of a great divergence
from the teachings of the Roman Church. Furthermore, former habits of mind even when they
undergo important changes are bound to manifest their old tendencies occasionally, but the occasion should not be taken as a basis for generali-
zation. No, we beg to differ with Papini's critics
concerning his Catholic faith. His recent writings
are fundamentally Catholic and very much so.

Surely Papini's *Sant'Agostino*, his *Gli operai della vigna*, his *Dante vivo* cannot be inter-
preted as a denial of his conversion.

In *Gli operai della vigna* (Laborers in the
Vineyard), Papini says in the preface:

"You will see that choice has led me to
speak of only three types of men: saints, men who
sought sanctity, and artists. For I confess that in
my view the only people one can really admire

or tolerate in this world are saints and artists; those who imitate God and those who imitate the works of God. Only they have any commerce with the Eternal, and for that reason they rise above the head of wage earners and pleasure seekers. Saints try to guess the soul of the Eternal and to become unto Him; artists strive to reproduce His vesture."

Concerning Papini's conversion to Christianity we cannot but share Crespi's belief:

"Whether his conversion was more than a convulsion, whether his character has really been reshaped and reborn or has only changed the direction of his spites and likings, time alone will show. But it is unquestionable that in turning not merely to Christianity, which he had scarcely known before, but to Roman Catholicism he has not given way to a mere wave of weariness or disgust or to mere momentary spites. These may be real causes and ingredients, but they are subordinate to something far more important: to a deep-seated pity for the soul of man ensnared in its own evil doings and habits; a noble longing for its redemption from the superficial world of things and machinery, speech and comfort; a thirst for unity and communion transcending worldly causes of division among men; a real discovery of the best in traditional Christianity."

VII.

ARDENGO SOFFICI

It is difficult to give a clear picture of Ardengo Soffici. There are so many sides to him. He is the most fascinating and likeable personalities it has been our privilege to know in the field of contemporary Italian art and letters. Soffici is known as a poet, artist, essayist, art critic and a *raconteur par excellence*.

Born in 1879 in Rignano, on the Arno, a small village not far from Florence, he has developed an artistic mentality and expression that is very markedly Tuscan. A long sojourn in Paris as a young art student broadened his vision and at the same time served to sharpen and intensify the Italian and particularly the Tuscan colorings of it.

Soffici has such an intuitive sense of the grotesque that he can extract out of the dullest or the most commonplace experience in life its most interesting and amusing elements. Walking with him along a street in Florence he will often suddenly stop and call your attention to something that does not seem out of the ordinary and forthwith proceeds to reveal in his inimitable language the secret of its hidden charm. He seeks and enjoys the company of the uneducated laborer or peasant as well as that of the writer or intellectual. It is no wonder then, that Prezzolini in his delightful book *Amici* says that if he were to go on a trip or a hike he would rather go with Soffici than with any other person in Italy.

Papini perhaps has found the secret of Soffici's compelling personality in asserting that it lies in the varied and changing colors of his many aspects. For Soffici can be both democratic and aristocratic, religious and libertine, idealist and realist, provincial and cosmopolitan, pessimist as well as optimist. But there is a permanent quality that seems to join these opposite poles and it is art. Artistry permeates everything he does or writes.

Soffici's only creed in life is art. It is his only *raison d'etre*. But as the famous French critic, Benjamin Crémieux so well pointed out: [1] "there are in Soffici two distinct tendencies: the first is to express what there is unique in himself, with all his scruples and application of an artist; the other is to revolutionize Italian literature, to overthrow the current artistic régime. Distinct tendencies which in practice have revealed themselves contradictory." Hence we find Soffici before the war a follower and exponent in turn of Impressionism, Futurism, Cubism. Yet the net residue of all his work reveals a close adherence to the purest and most classical of Italian traditions. Soffici realizes the full value of the contrasts and paradoxes in which his early work abounds. He feels however that his present artistic outlook has been sharpened and enriched by these

---

[1] in *Revue de France,* Oct. 1, 1921, p. 633.

contrasts or contradictions which he feels are characteristic of nature itself.

On his return from his long period of study in France to the family residence at Poggio a Caiano near Florence, Soffici became shocked at the deplorable spiritual state into which his fellow countrymen had fallen. In 1911 he published a novel entitled *Lemmonio Boreo*. In it Lemmonio, the hero, after years spent in foreign lands, returns home to see his beloved Tuscany in the hands of charlatans, corrupted politicians and hypocritical officials. Turning to literature he discovers a prevalent worthlessness in everything he reads. The same discouraging insincerity he finds in the drama, poetry, art, philosophy. In bold fearless terms and with an occasional choice *parolaccia* after the manner of Papini, Soffici flays the artificiality, vulgarity and presumption of writers who have never seen anything, never felt anything, never loved, never suffered, who know nothing of art and differ only in the amount and kind of rubbish they disseminate. Deeply incensed at this state of affairs, Lemmonio sets out through a series of exciting and unusual adventures to redress wrongs, to combat hypocricies and to attempt to bring about a reform.

Soffici's very strong likes and dislikes are aired in no uncertain terms in *Lemmonio Boreo*. The novel however did not enjoy much popular success and fell short of the artistic standard set by the author. It helped, nevertheless, to arouse a number of Italians to the necessity of taking a more active part in the political and cultural life of their country and presaged the coming of

99

Fascism. It may be interesting to note that a few years later when Mussolini organized his paper the *Popolo d'Italia* he called upon Soffici to become one of his chief collaborators.

But to the student of contemporary Italian letters Soffici has much more to offer than *Lemmonio Boreo*. If one were to make a list of the more noteworthy literary productions of recent years in Italy, one would have to include the *Giornale di Bordo, Arlecchino, Kobilek,* not to mention such excellent critical studies as *Medardo Rosso, Scoperte e Massacri, Ricordi di Vita Artistica e Letteraria* and his recent *Arno Borghi,* in the style of the delightful *Giornale di Bordo.*

Kobilek is a calm, unadorned narrative of the battle on Mt. Kobilek where the author fought in the Great War and was twice wounded. It shows a Soffici no longer delighting in polemics, in artistic or literary discussions. Cynicism, derision, scorn for the lack of intelligence in his fellow men give way to a grave austerity, an affectionate fraternity, new and unexpected. With a somber spontaneity he records attacks, agonies, the horrors of the trenches, the incoherence of the combat. Before the war Soffici had been a pronounced internationalist. But in *Kobilek* Soffici sees things in a new light through closer contacts with his fellowmen. He comes to understand Italy's part in the World Struggle. He appreciates the warmhearted temperament of the common soldier, his boundless, exuberant passion for joy even when faced with the harshness and bitterness of many sacrifices. Unlike Remarque's "All Quiet on the Western Front," Soffici's *Kobilek* is devoid of propaganda either for or against war. What attracts the reader is the extremely modest role played by the author himself who is far from being a brave warrior or an ingenious military tactician. From a purely literary point of view *Kobilek* surpasses most of the war books published in Europe.

In *Giornale di Bordo*, a sort of diary or log of his most intimate thoughts, Soffici writes:

"I have experienced joy under all skies
    Blessed be life.
I have experienced sorrow under all skies
    Blessed be life."

"It is sad not to be understood: not for me, of course, but for those who do not understand me."

"I don't like to travel third class; in it one finds laborers, peasants, stupid, uneducated, ill-mannered and dirty people.

When, however, I think of the travelers in second and first class!—then I buy a third class ticket."

"Few like me, so much the worse for the many."

"It is perhaps less difficult to be a genius than to find one who is capable of recognizing it."

"In a tram — What a great imbecility is patriotism, after all. When I look at this corpulent perspiring Tuscan broker near me and feel I must consider him closer and more akin to me than the Frenchman who is the author of the book I have in my hand, the reflection of my most precious being, and that to save his hide and that of his

101

family I might to-morrow have to kill on a battlefield a Guillaume Apollinaire, a Max Jacob or my
friend Picasso!—"

Soffici first made himself really known to
readers in Italy when he joined Prezzolini and
Papini as a contributor to *La Voce*, the Florentine
weekly that was to exert much influence on the
subsequent trend of Italian cultural and political
life. The artistic knowledge and experience gathered during his several years sojourn in Paris made
Soffici realize also how much Italians were in
the dark concerning the new artistic tendencies in
Europe.

Through a series of very interesting articles
he began to enlighten readers on the new schools
of painting. He revealed to the Italian public the
works of Picasso and Renoir. He unveiled the
true merit of the paintings of Giovanni Fattori.
Furthermore, the first exposition in Italy of the
paintings of the most famous impressionists of
Europe was organized by him. It was held in
Florence, and Soffici with the help of his *Voce*
friends was able to secure and bring together for
exhibition works by Degas, Sisley, Cézanne, Van
Gogh, Gauguin, Pissarro, Picasso, Matisse, Forain
and others. At the same time a special exhibition
was held of the sculptures of Medardo Rosso
whose artistic merit, had it not been for Soffici,
would have long remained buried for Italians.

Arlecchino, considered by some critics as Soffici's literary masterpiece, is a short collection of
beautiful impressionistic literary images written
during the period of *La Voce*. These choice fragments, as rich in color as the palette of the artist,
contain word pictures of his Tuscany in the dif-

ferent seasons of the year. We go through a delightful series of sharply outlined and varied colored *ceichés* of peasants, of their poor squallid homes, of their attachment to the soil. We learn that Soffici's two favorite and most sacred odors are the smell of warm bread just out of the oven and the fragrance of earth recently soaked by rain. We follow Soffici on his solitary rambles through paths and by-ways where he communes with nature at all hours and in all moods; we accompany him on rail journeys, giving vivid snapshots of the fleeting landscape through a car window. We walk with Soffici along a street of Florence or sit with him at some Florentine café. *Arlecchino* also contains a hint of the gay bragadoccio and a thread of the light cynicism that are so characteristic of Soffici when he discourses on the egoism of human nature, on love, art, morality, immorality.

In order, however, to fully appreciate Soffici the artist, one must know Soffici the man. Although Soffici claims that life is a continuous failure—*(la vita è un fallimento continuato)* the reader of his books knows him to be exquisitely happy in being alive with a great capacity for joy even in meager circumstances.

Soffici maintains that affluence restrains the development of talent. In *Giornale di Bordo* he alludes to a young artist who first complained that without the same economic pressure he would not have attained the greatness that he possessed. According to Soffici, to achieve eminence in any line man needs to struggle, to acquire the consciousness of accomplishment. More than that, he must be severe with himself.

103

"If you complain, you are a coward. Be severe with yourself and with others, but more with yourself . . . in order that you may be stronger and nobler."

In *Taccuino di Arno Borghi* (Firenze, Vallecchi 1933), Soffici smacks of the Latin Quarter of Paris and at the same time smells of ploughed ground. He opens his store of memories, puts on display love-letters, unfinished articles, notes, sketches; he takes down a book from the shelves and makes comments on the writer; he sees a helmet and it recalls to him his impressions of the World War. You spend two hours, three hours, delighted, bewildered, astonished, asking yourself by what miracle in this amazing labyrinth you have found a thread and who was the Ariadne who handed it to you. Who is the Ariadne here? Soffici himself, with his engaging personality, the only one who could give unity to so much chaos.

Here are some of Soffici's characteristic pronouncements. With some you will readily agree, with others you may not—yet they are all worthy of thought and consideration if only because of the way Soffici expresses them.

"One thing that always astounds me is to see how men flee from these too apparent truths that would be their only guide through the sorrowful labyrinth in which they lose themselves. Try to tell some one these days, for instance, that all the woes of the world are caused by a lack of charity; and that every problem whether social, political, economic, and even esthetic would be quickly solved if there were a return to Catholic Christianity." [1]

"In a word the true stable unity of Europe can only be founded on a return to a Catholic Christianity (the anathema of materialism and of nationalistic ego and the propounder of the love of charity and of political and social justice), and to a Latin universality (the enemy of abstract ideologies, of special oppressions and the bulwark of law and equity." [2]

"The need of God is reborn in our hearts— God is therefore rising again. The birth of God means the death of art without God—it means the death of all "modern" art. There will remain only that art that was performed for all times— neither modern nor ancient—as God himself." [3]

"Every true artist, to create effectively, has need of believing himself greater than all his living companions. But he must not say it. Not even to himself." [4]

"The ancient world is dead, solely because of the powerless. Virile and really creative youth draws from the tombs inspiration, enthusiasm and models of glory. The sacred dust of the dead worlds has an inebriating scent almost as if the new being breathed the vital essence of his fore-fathers, the powerful smell of their blood saturat-ed from ancient sepulchres, from the ruins and remains of ideal civilization. The great men of that period were spurred on to sublime efforts through their link with their dead ancestors: they

[1] Page 15, *Taccuino* di Arno Borghi.
[2] Page 298, *Ibid*.
[3] Page 315, *Ibid*.
[4] Page 46, *Ibid*.

acquired fertile pride and joy. Italy would not be what she is or what she will be if she had not kept sacred and worshipped the memory of the dead ages and especially of the culture of ancient Rome." [5]

"I have never read a book of adventure in my life. I have had many of them and I think that is better." [6]

When reproached by the critics for his *frammentarismo*, Soffici replied that all great works are composed of flawless *frammenti* (fragments) intermixed with imperfections. So after all, he asks, is not a small perfect work preferable to a large and faulty one?

Soffici delights in the perception of every shade and nuance of color. He speaks of "the green sky, the white rain, the ashen clouds, the orange shadows, the blue thickets, the shrubbery black under a midnight fire." He also has a Baudelarian flair for odors: "The fresh fragrance of soil after a heavy rain. The smell of an old goat. The perfume of the star-filled sky. The strong odor of warm flesh and wine laden breaths in a crowd."

Nature has a vibrant soul with which he is in perfect accord, so perfect that Soffici sometimes resents the intervention of poetry. "I often feel too much of a poet to like poetry. Nature speaks to me so affectionately that the introduction of any art between me and her seems to disturb, obscure and falsify our communion."

---

5   Page 133, *Ibid*.
6   Page 69, *Ibid*.

Because his artist's soul is so keenly sensitive, so abundantly alive, no detail of his surroundings escapes Soffici. In fact, the small things are for him the great, the significant things. The shining flight of an insect, a step in the night, a drop of water reflecting the sky, these are of utmost importance. Sitting in the open square of an old Tuscan village surrounded by happy children at play, while the setting sun reveals the brilliant splendor of age-old houses rich in golden windows, Soffici feels that life is complete and for the moment at least he can ask for nothing more.

VIII.

ALDO PALAZZESCHI

Aldo Palazzeschi is considered by discerning critics of Italian letters among the greatest writers in Italy today, if not one of the more unusual, interesting and representative figures in contemporary European literature. Benjamin Crémieux, widely known French critic of present-day Italian literary works, calls Palazzeschi *l'enfant moderne, très malicieux, spirituel, goguenard.* It was Crémiuex also who first hailed Palazzeschi as the "only true poet of fantasy that Italy has had since 1870."

Palazzeschi was born in Florence in 1885. As a boy he attended the commercial schools of his native city. Manifesting in his early youth a marked predilection for letters, he was not long in becoming interested in the new Futuristic school of poetry that was gaining a strong foothold in Italy during the years 1908 and 1909. He produced his first volume of poems about this time. It was entitled *L'Incendario.* The publisher of his first volume of verse was Cesare Blanc. At the time readers did not know who Cesare Blanc was. Much surprise was expressed that a new publisher had ventured into the Italian book market, but the surprise was even greater when, upon inquiry, it was discovered that Palazzeschi's publisher was none other than his pet cat, Cesare Blanc.

Was it Pascoli who said that a man could never be a poet unless he retained something of the child's propensity for the fantastic or the imaginative in life? When we became personally acquainted with Palazzeschi in Florence several years ago we were convinced that this unusual European writer possesses this quality to a striking degree. Upon closer acquaintance with his works and with his charming personality, it appeared to us that Palazzeschi, like the young boy, can often be in a gay, mischievous mood.

His early poems are crepuscular in character. It is difficult to determine their exact meaning. It is even more difficult to distinguish the sentiment that inspired them. In this category we would place such poems as: *Ara Mara Amara, Il Segno* and *Oro Doro Odoro Dodoro*. When, however, we come to poems like *Rio Bo, Chi Sono?, Lo Specchio,* and *La Fontana Malata* we are aware that the haze in the earlier compositions has been lifted and the reader finds himself before a clear, limpid, stream of unquestionable artistic inspiration.

With apologies to our good friend, Aldo Palazzeschi, we offer here our versions in English of *Chi Sono?* (Who am I?) and *La Fontana Malata* (The Sick Fountain), two of his most characteristic poetic compositions.

WHO AM I?

Who am I?
Am I perhaps a poet?
No certainly.
The pen of my soul
writes but one strange word:
folly.
Am I then a painter?
Not even.
There is but one color
on the palette of my soul:
melancholy.
A musician then?
Not at all.
There is but one note
on the keyboard of my soul:
nostalgia.
I am then . . . what?
I place a lens
before my heart,
so that all may see.
Who am I?
I am the mountebank of my soul.

THE SICK FOUNTAIN

Clop, clop, cloch,
cloffete
cloppete
clocchete
ch ch ch . . .
Down there
in the courtyard
the poor
sick
fountain,
what anguish
to hear
it cough!
It coughs,
and coughs,
then silent
a while,
then again
it coughs.
My poor
sick
fountain,
your great
distress
my heart
oppresses.
Its silent,
no more
that spitting,
no sound
of any kind,

has it
perhaps
perhaps
died?
Horrors!
No!
There's
that cough
again.
Clop, clop, cloch,
cloffete
cloppete
clocchete
ch ch ch . . .
It's dying
of consumption.
Oh Lord!
That cough
eternal
is simply
infernal.
A little
all right,
but
so much . . .
Wailing.
Oh Children!
children!
Run,
go
and shut

that fount!
Its persistent
cough
is killing
me.
Run,
go
and stop
that sigh.
even
even
if it
must die.
Heavens!
No more!
No more!
My poor
sick
fountain
your
anguish,
you'll see,
will also
be
the end
of
me.
Clop, clop, cloch
cloffete
clocchete
ch ch ch . . .

In 1914 Palazzeschi's infatuation with the Futuristic Muse began to grow less warm. His subsequent publications reveal an artistic attitude of mind that is free and independent of all schools of literary thought. The obscurity in his early "Twilight Poems" has vanished. He relates how his first literary efforts were received with a few choice jeers and how, as the sound of the jeering spread, it gradually lost its intensity. In 1913, with the appearance of the second edition of his poems, not only did the jeering cease but he even heard an occasional shout of approval. Since then he says he has not been jeered any more. In answer to a query as to what he would do in the future, Palazzeschi replied in his own characteristic way: "Either I shall work to provoke new jeers or I shall strive to lay the foundation for real admiration."

In his works Palazzeschi expresses a delicacy of pathos and a melancholy sweetness that are rare in contemporary literature. Ardengo Soffici, well-known Italian artist, author and critic, knew no bounds of praise when he claimed that Palazzeschi in his more successful works surpasses Carducci, Pascoli and D'Annunzio, even going so far as to say that he is "the first who, after Leopardi, has known how to translate for us the visions , the emotions and the new palpitations of our modern life."

But there is something more to the poetic atmosphere of Palazzeschi than the simple, fresh and melancholy air of his poems. A reading of such important prize works as *La Piramide, Le Sorelle Materassi, Stampe dell'ottocento* and

113

his recent *Palio dei Buffi,* reveals the fact that there is in this "poeta pura" a strong undercurrent of subtle humor and delicious irony. Palazzeschi is frequently perplexed and at the same time amused by the impenetrable incongruities and paradoxes of life. Society for him assumes at times the aspect of a large three ring circus and like a youngster attending his first performance he laughs heartily at the antics of the clowns before him. At the height of his gay mood everything seems to strike him in a humorous vein and his most hearty chuckles are elicited by the somersaults of poets and the tight rope walking of philosophers. To cap the climax the laughing spell only ends when for some reason or other Palazzeschi stops suddenly and realizes what a ridiculous figure he too has been cutting. And there is one more hearty laugh but this time it is at himself.

Take for example *Il Codice di Perelà,* perhaps the most fantastic, eccentric, and entertaining novel that has been produced in Italy in the last fifty years.

In Perelà we find Palazzeschi writing to amuse himself. He is in one of his most mischievous and light moods. The story deals with the humorous and tragic experiences in a modern society of a guileless and fantastic creature named Perelà, who is made of smoke. The adventures of Perelà, portrayed mostly in dialogue form, offer Palazzeschi an opportunity to reveal to us the inconsistencies of our loves and hates, our likes and dislikes. He seems to be amused at the exaggerated manner in which we humans take ourselves seriously—whether the all-important problem of the moment be one of politics, economics, war, love, sex, poetry, religion, or philosophy. We all have a role to play in the drama of life, but most of us seem predisposed to laugh at others, forgetting that if the spotlight were turned on ourselves we might be found to be cutting up even funnier capers. Perelà, upon meeting the National Poet, Mr. Isidor Littlebroom, inquires innocently:

"And what is poetry?"

"Poetry, Mr. Perelà, is a world, it is a globe all blue, and the breath which inflates it and prepares it for its celestial ascent is the poet on Parnassus. What is art? It is to know how to inflate it, to swell it to the point of making it transparent so that it can rise."

"And do you go up with it afterwards?"

"Not at all! A foreign body? If I attach myself to it, good Lord, it would remain down on earth. When I have inflated it, I send it off. I remain on Parnassus."

"You must then watch it carefully when you blow it up—your globe—so that nothing goes into it?"

"Why, of course. A grain of the simplest matter, and it would not go up any more. It looks as though there might be something in it, but instead there is nothing. To obtain emptiness, that is the art of the poet and of poetry.

"I shall compose for you an ode of thirteen thousand endecasyllabic verses and a dactylic septenary and I shall send it to you published in the best periodical of the country.

"Here is my last book of verse: *Sick Ballads.*"

"Oh! What a pity, poor things!"

"Don't become afflicted."

"And of what malady do they suffer?"

"None—they are very well."

"Then why did you say they were sick?"

"Otherwise no one could care about their health, that is the way of the world, Signor Perelà. You may count upon my friendship, and I hope to be able to count upon yours. We are, after all, two poets, and we can write a dramatic poem in collaboration."

"Soon after I leave, the critic, Mr. Constantine-the-Fish will come, and I beg you not to listen to a single word of what he will have to say. The lazy good-for-nothing is waiting outside the door, and is watching until I take my leave so as to be able to speak to you without doubt about me, the parasite."

"Monsieur de Perelà j'espère de vous rencontrer dans le monde."

"Mr. Constantine-the-Fish, official critic of the national literature."

"Don't be surprised if I am introduced to you after that good-for-nothing. Fate decreed that he be given precedence over me, but that will not happen much longer. Ere long you will see a reversal of things."

"Who? That fellow of the balloon?"

"Exactly, just he, he can well expect to sing after I have spoken. It won't be difficult to guess what nonsense he will speak."

116

"And does he make you see it inflated or still to be inflated?"

"What?"

"The balloon."

"He makes me see it inflated."

"And do you have to go up there where he sends it—the balloon?"

"I have my field glasses. Don't you know about the field glasses of the critic? They are the longest of all and at the same time the ones that can best retract. I carry them in my vest pocket, see." [1]

[1] For the complete English version of *Il Codice di Perelà* see *Perelà, the Man of Smoke,* adapted from the Italian of Aldo Palazzeschi by Peter M. Riccio (S. F. Vanni, New York, 1936.)

IX.

ALFREDO PANZINI

Upon the publication of his delightful critical essays entitled *Stroncature,* Giovanni Papini regretted that he had never met Alfredo Panzini face to face. Having read Panzini's early compositions he felt that here was a writer that one could not only admire and appreciate but also love, " . . . really love," writes Papini, "as if he were some one we knew even if he were not the producer of books. Panzini is not only a great prose-writer and an artist who without effort can find all the charm which an ironical elegance can contribute to the ornamentation of a page or a chapter, but also a wonderful fellow, who reveals himself and arouses your sympathy with printed words as others might with a simple conversation over the table or on the street. Panzini would be an admirable fellow, if he were merely a writer, but his writings reveal him to be a man, and therefore he is also lovable."

Panzini was born the same year as D'Annunzio (1863) in the province of Romagna. Although he belongs to the generation of Italy's Soldier-Poet his writings must be classified as post-Dannunzian. He first studied in Venice and later in Bologna under Carducci, whose influence left its imprint on his early works. For many years he taught letters and history at the Politecnico of Milan and then transferred to Rome where he has been living ever since.

Throughout the first decade of the present century Panzini was relatively unknown though he had already published a half dozen works, among which were *Il libro dei morti* (1893); *L'evoluzione di Giosuè Carducci* (1894); *Piccole storie del mondo grande* (1901); *Trionfi di donna* (1903); and *Le fiabe della virtù* (1905). With the publication of *La lanterna di Diogene* in 1909 the literary group of *La Voce* brought Panzini into the public eye as a writer of unmistakable promise and elegance.

As a teacher Panzini was soon disillusioned by the relatively insignificant role that letters play in bourgeois existence. He was startled to discover how little adapted to life were the intellectuals of his day. Panzini could not tolerate the acceleration in materialistic living brought about by new inventions, by new styles in dress, or by the migrations to urban centers of peasants trained in traditional and patriarchal agriculture. Hence we find him inveighing against silk stockings, bobbed hair, speeding autos, express elevators. Yet this lover of Plato and Socrates is not entirely convincing as a critic of modernity.

It is not because Panzini has not caught up with modernity but rather because modernity has speeded past him — beyond his reach. This may explain the malicious flavor that is so character-

istic of his humor. Panzini prefers the reposeful
ideals of the old faiths to the vertiginous and
aimless existence of this age. Yet when he be-
rates contemporary life Panzini has his tongue in
his cheek and it is with difficulty that he refrains
from laughing at himself. Although he decries
silk stockings you feel that he might be among
the first to stop and admire a young girl in silk
stockings crossing a street. He abhors those who
attach much importance to money. Yet when we
first became acquainted with him several years
ago in the Ufficio Bibliografico of Rome, among
the first questions he asked us was: "What is the
salary of high school teachers in New York?"
When we told him, his eyes sparkled, his face
beamed, and he said "How I would like to teach
in New York!"

But whether Panzini is lauding the simple, rustic life of a peasant family or berating the dizzy
faithless existence of a bourgeois the reader is
treated to a remarkable display of literary skill.
Panzini is an erudite man of letters whose style is
pungent with refreshing humor and delightful
satire. In "Diogene's Lantern," which is unques-
tionably his masterpiece, Panzini takes us on a
sentimental bicycle journey through Italy. It was
Renato Serra, the late critic, who said that in this
remarkable volume one will find pages that Carducci forgot to write. In it Panzini gives a beautiful picture of Italy, its marvelous climate, its gor-
geous landscapes, its remarkable cuisine, its joy-
ful children, its many artistic monuments.

It is, however, in the company of simple folk
and at the sight of an old stone farm house, un-

spoiled by the inroads of modernity, that Panzini warms to his task. Thirsty and tired from cycling one day, he describes how he stops at a little farm house and knocks at the door. Of the peasant woman who opens he inquires:

"Could you let me have some milk, please?"
"We brought it all to the cheese-maker."
"Is he far from here?"
"Up there on the summit where you see those houses."

Panzini, too fatigued to proceed to the summit, bows his head and inquires further:

"Would you mind letting me in to change my undershirt?"

" 'Certainly!' she replied and stepped back so that I might enter; and as I did so I realized that 'certainly' really meant 'certainly not', but how can one refuse a human kindness? Since I did not wish to appear before her after the manner in which Ulysses presented himself to the beautiful Nausica, I therefore asked her for a room. Having rendered one human service it was now necessary to render another (often it is necessary to render a third; perhaps that is the reason so many people deny a first favor).

"Well, let us tip the good peasant wife for her kindness! She refused. I insisted; and in accepting she remembered that, while she had no more milk, she had some fresh eggs; and since there was a fire she could even make me some coffee! She preceded me into the kitchen and offered me a chair.

122

"The sun beat through the little kitchen where everything was spic and span; the sun's rays refracted on the kitchen utensils over the fire-place. The only sound was the somnolent buzzing of some big flies.

"She had put the coffee-pot on the fire, dropped the fresh yellowish pearl of two eggs into a clean cup, sprinkled the sugar with frugality, and then started to whip with much dexterity.

'Where did you learn to do things so well?'

'I was a house-maid, Sir, for twenty years.'

'Then you married?'

'Yes, Sir.'

'And you have children?'

"Yes, Sir. But they are not here because in the mountains only the old folks remain; I have one son, working in Switzerland, and a daughter who is a housemaid in Turin."

'And your husband?'

'My husband is busy harvesting.'

'On your own land?'

'Yes, Sir, but it is just a handful of dirt, hardly enough to bury us.'

"And is this house your own?'

'These few stones? Yes, Sir, they are ours.

"Up to this point she had replied as if I were a federal tax agent, but when I asked her the all-important question:

'In short, you are happy?'

'Oh, happy!' she said. 'Well, we live tranquilly!'

"As if to live tranquilly were not happiness! And I felt like levying an enormous tax on that tranquility."

123

Panzini's bicycle journey as described in *La lanterna di Diogene* takes him from Milan across the Apennines to Bellaria on the sea. We find Panzini desirous of "levying enormous taxes" on a number of things, and on a number of people, not excluding Panzini himself, perhaps.

The book sparkles with humor. One of the most delightful extracts is one in which he describes how, one morning, while cycling through a country road his attention is attracted by some large beautiful oak trees. He stops to rest a while and to enjoy the beauties of nature. After the manner of Saint Francis, Panzini feels the urge to thank Mother Earth, and Father Sun for their blessings. He hears the enchanting song of a little bird perched on the branch of an oak tree and wishes that the flowers, the birds, and the trees might take him into their company.

Turning to the bird perched on the oak tree Panzini, thinking aloud, says:

"Brother bird! Sister oak! gather me unto your fold!"

"Brother man!" replies the bird, "You can't fool us; for, when your enthusiasm is cooled, you have the habit of cooking us n a spit!"

And with a thrill of fear the bird flies away.

This incident serves as an excellent setting for the subsequent humorous developments of that day's journey. When our author decides to stop at an inn for a meal the waiter asks him what he would like to order and Panzini is indeed disconcerted to find, among the specialties of the day, birds on the spit. Then noticing over the fire the drooping heads of the little beasts revolving on a spit, he is reminded of Brother Bird on the oak whom he had loved early that morning. Unable to withstand the temptation of such a tasty dish Panzini begins to reason thus:

"Furthermore it is an error of simple judgment to suppose that little animals do not seek their vengeance. Microbes get together by the million, build their deadly cities in our proud bodies while other myriads of microbes carefully prepare themselves under earth for our complete destruction.

"Even the vegetarians and ascetics cannot escape this sad and fatal destiny. Let us devour each other, therefore, without remorse and without pity, I concluded, sticking my fork into one of the bipeds."

Since the publication of *La lanterna di Diogene*, Panzini has published over a score of volumes but none have had the success of this delightful book. He has published a number of works on women, the most noteworthy being *Santippe* (1914) and *Io cerco moglie* (1920). He visualizes woman as the inspiration or the curse of man's existence. She is very little for herself. Of his other volumes. *Il viaggio di un povero letterato* (1919) and *Il diavolo nella mia biblioteca* (1921) are among the more successful.

Panzini has also published a Modern Dictionary, written in his characteristic humorous vein. Paradoxically enough it was an effort to bring the Italian vocabulary up to modern tastes and requirements. Besides some two score volumes Panzini has had time to do extra tutoring and lecturing, has collaborated on a number of reviews and newspapers, has published several school texts, grammars and readers. Is it any wonder that critics have said that Panzini has written too abundantly and commercialized his talents? Is it any wonder that the artistic level of his literary work has fallen off noticeably since the World War? But even though Panzini has been too prolific a writer, even though his humor since 1918 has turned somewhat sour, no one can deny the superlative literary qualities of such volumes as *La lanterna di Diogene, Il viaggio di un povero letterato,* and *Santippe.*

Unlike his contemporary, Giovanni Papini, who was also bewildered by the present age of aimless living, Panzini's dissatisfaction is expressed not in the boisterous, unchanneled and outspoken phrases of the former, but in the mild, suave, and satirical manner of the old professor who loves to admonish his pupils on the dangers of the new life that lies ahead.

He is an outstanding interpreter of the clash between the old and the new in Italy — an interpreter whose humor and humanity are bound to give joy and light to future generations of readers.

X.

MASSIMO BONTEMPELLI

Massimo Bontempelli (born at Como, in 1878) professor, journalist, short-story writer, established in 1926 a review entitled: *Novecento*. It was to manifest objectively the tendencies of twentieth century life, to be anti-sentimental, anti-traditional and ultra-intellectual. Having for so many years leaned toward the classical and traditional in letters, Bontempelli felt it was time for a change.

His first works reveal a post-Carduccian style and like every good Carduccian he alternates poetry and the novel with criticism and with the practice of translation. The Futurist wave envelopes him fully in *La vita intensa* (Florence 1920) but Futurism for this unrequited writer only represents a moment of transition.

The concept of art as a game could not find for itself a more characteristic, demonstrative or ingenuous example than Bontempelli. Literature becomes a pastime, a trifling amusement, with a technique that is highly individualized and inimitable. Bontempelli, who has not the gift of profound passion nor of exquisiteness, is always ready to gather and utilize the new currents in literary taste, to carry them to extremes and to give to them the character of refined, terse and conscious absurdity.

In his *Primi Racconti* (Milano, Mondadori, 1934) Bontempelli offers a variety of short stories colored with strange implications. He treats common-place events with such exaggeration and distortion of logic that he seems to evolve a more vivid reality. In the first part of this collection, under the title of *Socrate moderno*, he dramatizes the rural schoolmaster's life. He shows how the ambition and individuality of the teacher are slowly but irretrievably lost in monotonous, unstimulating surroundings and in petty duties. The predominant note is one of disillusionment.

Bontempelli turns to a humorous hallucination, of a strange flavor, which derives from what might be called the dramatization of sophism. His characters are not men, but the premises, major and minor, and the conclusions of apparently irreprehensible sophisms, and they serve to give a bitterly exasperating tone to his humor.

Of the works of Bontempelli, let us examine *La vita intensa,* and *La vita operosa,* since they are, in our opinion, the most representative. The author shows himself to be the possessor of that rare gift in all literature — the gift of humor. It is an infectious humor, of a subtle kind. Fantastic stories are written about the most trivial of things, and about almost nothing at all, for the author has a good fund of words to expend on matters comically ponderous and delightfully evanescent. Cats, salmon, cigarettes, music lessons, and a poker game that will win the affection of every good card-player . . . these are his subjects, and they are treated with such good-natured, hilarious lunacy, that the bewildered reader is forced reluctantly to the belief that either the author is slightly mad, or that he himself (the reader) is becoming somewhat unbalanced!

In his preface the author acknowledges: "I do not write for those men who are too simple," and a few lines further down the page: "And I do not write for those men who are too complicated. I write for posterity. I write to renew the European romance." Truly a large ambition!

Again we find: "This romance has no preface, because there is no need of it," as the opening for a preposterous story of a jealous lady — Marta Calabieri, and for its conclusion, the author writes naively: "This romance has no conclusion, because there is no need of one."

Perhaps the most satisfying of all the stories in *La vita intensa* is the description of the poker-game which commences with the internationally-known warning: One hour of play, and no more!

"No game of poker has ever lasted less than six or seven hours: the players all know this, and that phrase has for none of them any value as a measure of time, or as a preventive precaution. But it is a formula, unremitting, ritual and traditional. Woe to the players who do not utter it: it may bring disaster! Every time in this vast world that there has been started a poker-game without that phrase, at the end some one of the players has had to regret it."

The stakes are decided upon in this manner. One writes on a small card ten lire, another one lira, the third five lire, and the fourth (the author himself) writes *one penny*. These cards are mixed scrupulously, and placed in a vase high above the players' heads. The game proceeds, the movements of the gambling symphony being appropriately marked: *Andante lento, Allegro agitato, Crescendo solenne e Stretta Finale.* The vase is solemnly taken down and the fatal card is drawn out, to determine the amount lost or won, but the author, in a fine burst of "leg-pulling", with equal solemnity declines to announce the winning ticket!

In *La vita operosa,* the fantastic sense of irresponsibility persists, but it must be acknowledged that without a fitting climax being reached, it becomes a little monotonous, rather in the manner of a comedian who remains on the stage and in the scene after his laughs have been won and his material is exhausted. His style, extravagant in burlesque, reminds one of Stephen Leacock, the Canadian humorist, in "Frenzied Fiction", or of A. A. Milne, the delightful British writer, in "Not That It Matters."

A delightfully simple method of art criticism is exposed in another chapter. Instead of confessing, "I don't understand paintings", there is a way less humiliating.

"Pay attention — continued Valacarda — that every once in a while you refurnish yourself with substantives and with adjectives. Before the war there were the words: "sensibility", "dynamic" and "musical": today instead the basic pillars of the critical vocabulary are "constructed", "fleshy", and "architecture". A vocabulary of

130

this type will last from three to five years. Until a few years ago the words "joy of living" were much used."

After riding around in a carriage for the greater part of a morning in an effort to find Via Bellovese, a non-existent street in Milan, another character observes:

"Deaf-mute, may you be blessed now and for always for that word. The Milanese — and he indicated with his hands outstretched, the backbone of the driver, the tail of the horse, the pavement, the house facing him, the passing crowd — the Milanese are all deaf and dumb. They do not know who Bellovese was. Bellovese was the Romulus and Remus of Milan. The Gaul, Bellovese, sir, was a nephew of a king of Biturigi, who almost six hundred years before Christ crossed the Alps and here encamping himself founded the city of Milan, the moral capital of Italy. And in Milan no one, no one knows it. In Milan there is not a road, a café, a school, a disorderly house, that is dedicated to the name of Bellovese. Let us get down, Signor. Will you pay the carriage or shall I?"

A further delightful inconsequentiality occurs on page 150:

"If up to now the reader of the present chapter has not read the six that precede it, it does not matter: for the information of these it is sufficient to know that on the morning of the 9th of February, at the hour of ten forty-five I had a headache."

It is small wonder that Pietro Pancrazi says that Bontempelli is "born to letters with nothing to say. . . From time to time he has sought to give himself a literary contest, to assume a part, or he has ironically turned back on his nothingness, on his poverty. . . One sees that Bontempelli intimately renounces the claims of futurism; his logic mad and empty, his insane classicism, his speculative sophism, must make of him a master and brother of the cubists."

In spite of this severe appraisal on the part of Pancrazi we feel however that Massimo Bontempelli has added to the gaiety of the nations in his lighter works, and for this slight relief, in this grey, work-a-day world, we should at least render him suitable thanks.

XI.

ANTONIO BALDINI

After the World War a group of young men headed by Vincenzo Cardarelli published in Rome *La Ronda,* a monthly literary review which lasted about four years (1919-1923). The young men did not wish to renounce any impartiality which was a condition of their liberty yet they wanted to repudiate the sordid impartialities and the vain liberty from which there did not emerge an ideal law and a technical discipline. Hence it was natural that they should seek inspiration from the works of Leopardi. Among these young men were Emilio Cecchi, the critic; Riccardo Bacchelli, Bruno Barilli, Armando Spadini, and Antonio Baldini, the most easy-going of friends and the most jealous of writers.

Baldini spent his early youth, an apathetic son of the family, always dreaming of poetry, casting aside any idea of practical employment, content to turn over pages of old and good books, elaborating or polishing literary forms. In a few years he developed a mature and impeccable style which revealed an instinctive and particular humor. And it is this humor, a humor that lives by its own nature, by instinct, that distinguishes Baldini from all the other writers in Italy today.

Baldini sees modernity, contemporaneity, in the light of the pale eternity in which he feels his temperament motivated. The contrast between the tremendously absorbing, crushing, daily realities and the distrait, distant and profound literary thoughts which these realities provoke gives true value to Baldini's humor. But it is a humor which also has a base of lyric melancholy and of tragic suffering.

The three works that to us are most representative of Baldini are *Michelaccio, La dolce calamità,* and *Amici allo spiedo.*

Michelaccio is a very amusing story of a bad boy. It symbolizes perhaps the natural laziness and mischievousness of Baldini himself. Michelaccio loves to eat, to sleep and to drink. So does Baldini. Michelaccio loves women. So does Baldini. Michelaccio is lazy. So is Baldini. But here —we agree with his critic Pancrazi—the analogy must end, for the laziness of Michelaccio is one thing while that of Baldini is a mode of being and of thinking—it is a style, a philosophy.

Baldini writes books, is the editor of *La nuova antologia,* is a lecturer and the father of a family. He found time to go to war and to bring back a medal. He was a merchant in Upper Silesia; and in all these years Baldini has always given the impression of not doing anything. Why? Because his greatest work consists actually in pretending not to work.

The story of Michelaccio begins thus: "Michelaccio was born at eleven months, without crying, one Sunday in sweet April—in a house exposed to the sun, on the bank of a canal. He was big, ruddy, hairy. His eyes were half shut and he whined like a dog on a chain.

"His father said: Look at that *pappalasagne!* and from the joy of having a male heir he was drunk for three days. His mother, upon giving him a breast feeding, suffered such untold anguish that in a few weeks she died. Whereupon the father went off on another drunk which lasted six days.

"In the meantime the young rascal sprouted two teeth and ate boiled turnips. He was never heard to shriek or to say gu! gu! like other children. He was never seen to weep except from his nose."

Baldini then goes on to tell how one day Michelaccio's father, after another drinking bout, fell into a canal. Whereupon Michelaccio's uncle, Salerno, a bandit and spendthrift, attracted to the boy because of his apparent dumbness, decided to look after him for his own ends. Everybody believed that Michelaccio was deaf and dumb but one night on the roof of Uncle Salerno's house there fell a thunderbolt. Uncle Salerno jumped up and sat on the bed, scared to death. Then there was heard for the first time the voice of Michelaccio: "Uncle, don't worry about it!" And this was the first of the memorable sayings of Michelaccio. The rest you will find in this story along with the other extraordinary facts of his life: Michelaccio in love, Michelaccio a soldier, on the field at Villanova, in prison, and in wedlock with the aged Marchesa di Bellamagione, who one night, unable to keep to herself the secret of the forthcoming addition to the family, arouses Michelaccio and announces abruptly: "There are now three of us." Michelaccio, startled, jumps out of bed and in a menacing tone shouts: "Who goes there?"

In *La dolce calamita* (The Sweet Magnet) Baldini gives amusing portraits of the women he has known and of the women he would like to have known. He says: "We live only once and I would not wish to leave this scene without having looked sufficiently long at the ladies. . . . I live, therefore, with my eyes open and at all times I seek to stamp them on my memory as much as I can." This was the origin of *La dolce calamita.* According to Baldini, the tools used in constructing this novel were his eyes and his memory, but as Pancrazi suggests, also a good portion of Baldini's phantasy and even abstraction entered into it.

The book is extremely entertaining in spite of its highly artificial atmosphere. It is full of *double entente, bon mots* and literary nuances. It is a book that only a stylist like Baldini would write.

In *Amici allo spiedo* (Friends on the Spit) Baldini rakes over the coals many of the leading contemporary literary and artistic luminaries. But the jabs are those of a friend—given in the spirit of good natured fun; for Baldini must have his fun, even at the expense of his most intimate colleagues. He gives indelible portraits of Malaparte, Bacchelli, Soffici, Papini, Giuliotti, Oppo, Spadini, De Chirico, Barilli, Beniamino (De Ritis), Frate Silvio (D'Amico), Ojetti, Civinini, Beltramelli, Simoni, Panzini, Don Benedetto (Croce);

to each he dedicates a few paragraphs or a chapter, a remembrance or a criticism, varying the tone and the music, but without ever forgetting the pinch of good humor—the *pizzicata.*

Of Malaparte, whose original name was Suckert, he writes: "this turbulent writer who has not succeeded in remaining at peace, not even with his own name." According to Baldini, "Bacchelli is a writer who every once in a while has many more things to say than the understanding strictly needs. When Bacchelli poises himself for a flight, nobody knows where he is going to a-light."

The art of writing, in Baldini's opinion "is more one of digging than of placing." His works reveal this conscious maxim. He wonders, also if he himself does not do "as the little boys do who lick off the marmalade and throw away the slice of bread."

At times Baldini displays an inordinate facility for making a literary mountain out of a commonplace molehill. He often takes a tiny point or a trivial incident and stretches it over a dozen printed pages, rather in the manner of the popular P. G. Wodehouse or the equally—but in a different direction—whimsical A.A. Milne. Critics have wished that Baldini had more faith in himself; a pinch more of courage would well become him. There can be no doubt that a certain verbal excellence weighs him down and that good literature has made him indolent. He is like an expert swimmer who does not wish to go out beyond the ropes.

The question is whether this lack of courage

and overabundance of rhetorical nuances are re-deemed by Baldini's gift of sparkling and delight-ful humor which flows through the books he has managed to complete. After reading the works in question we are rather forced to the conclusion that they certainly are. One is bound to like Bal-dini, not in spite of, but because of his indolence, his gluttony, his love of comfort.

XII.

DINO CAMPANA

The recent death of Dino Campana in the insane asylum of Castel Pucci closes one of the most romantic chapters in the history of contemporary Italian letters. Certainly no more unfortunate, eccentric, irascible, fantastic and at the same time artistically gifted individual ever graced the literary stage of twentieth century Italy. Page Pirandello! Here is a real subject for the study of multiple personalities.

A subversive and a reactionary, an anarchist and an imperialist, Dino Campana was a man of very versatile, strange and complex make-up. He could be as docile as he was violent in temper. At times he was a veritable mad-man. Late in life, when he became obsessed with the idea that he was being continuously persecuted, he reminds us of a Tasso in modern dress. Is it any wonder that his whole life smacks of strangeness, mystery, legend?

There is little documentary evidence in Italy concerning the literary activity of Dino Campana. It was by pure accident that we became acquainted with his sparse writings. One day at Soffici's home at Poggio a Caiano we were rummaging among some bookshelves when we came across the original manuscript of *Canti Orfici*. Looking over the pages of the quaint manuscript we began reading the beautiful fragmentary compositions in prose and poetry. As we were noticing a quotation from Nietzche on one page and another from Soffici on art, Soffici himself entered the room. Glancing at the manuscript we were reading and apparently aware that we were engrossed in it, Soffici drew a chair near the fireplace and nodded for us to sit down. From the strange tale that Soffici told us and from bits of information obtained in conversation with others who knew Campana we gathered together the following data:

Dino Campana was born at Marradi, a small town about fifty kilometers north of Florence. From early childhood he gave evidence of peculiar traits of character. The townspeople of Marradi spoke of him as the "figlio strambo del signor direttore delle Scuole." As a young man he became interested in chemistry and for a time studied at the university of Bologna, but his propensity for alchemy contained nothing of the cold and positive character of the scientist. Like Shelley, Campana's alchemistic dreams and experiments soon threw his room and his roommates into a turmoil of activity. He tried to perform the n ost unusual of experiments and attempted to preach the most unorthodox of ideas, with the same ultimate result — expulsion from the university. Then Campana began a series of wanderings to distant lands in Europe, in North America, in South America, then back again to Europe. He pursued many trades and gained a most unusual culture., He struggled with starvation and endured many bitter experiences. He became a modern Ulysses whose journeys took him to the haunts of gauchos, miners, gypsies, beggars, organ grinders, stokers, anarchists, mountebanks.

After his many peregrinations, Campana appeared again in Italy in 1913. One day he visited the printing establishment of Attilio Vallecchi in Florence and submitted a manuscript containing a collection of his writings. In the office of Vallecchi there were present at the time, Giovanni Papini and Ardengo Soffici. He entrusted his manuscript to them. Papini and Soffici, after reading a few selections, immediately recognized the poetic force of Campana and invited him to become a contributor to their famous review *Lacerba*.

Campana at this time was a man in his thirties, powerfully built, with ruddy complexion, reddish hair, a beard, and strikingly resembling the portrait of Rubens. Because of his adventurous spirit and his leaning towards mysticism, one might easily have taken him for a Nordic. Some claimed, however, that he looked more like a Slav. In spirit at any rate he was Italian and more specifically Romagnolo.

After his visit to Vallecchi's establishment Campana again disappeared mysteriously. After a long absence he returned to Florence. Then there began another series of trips at irregular intervals from his native town of Marradi to Florence and back. By this time the fame of his *Canti Orfici* had spread. Campana had finally found a printer in Marradi who would publish some copies of his poems. There was not enough of the same kind of paper to complete the printing of the first edition. When the edition appeared each copy was made up of two very different kinds of paper. With a few copies of his *Canti* under his arm Campana often journeyed on foot from his home to Florence, a distance of over thirty miles, in the hope of meeting someone who might purchase a copy. With the money obtained from the sales of his book he would live in Florence a few days. Then he would hike all night and practically all of the next day back to Marradi.

The Great War came. Campana had always been an admirer of the Germans, at least in a literary way, but with the opening of hostilities he turned vehemently against them. He became so enraged over the action of the Teutonic Powers that he used to go to Gonnelli's Book Shop in Via Ricasoli to look for the dedications he had written in books to German friends in order that he might erase them or tear out the pages on which they appeared. He volunteered to fight at the first opportunity. He was no sooner made a sergeant in the Italian army than he began to show unmistakable signs of mental disorders and was promptly discharged.

His conduct in the literary cafés now became more boisterous. He would start violent literary or political discussions that often resulted in fist fights. He would pick quarrels with coachmen, chauffeurs, street vendors. He would get into an argument with friends who had purchased a copy of his book by tearing selections from it while they were not looking and justified his action on the ground that they had no right to them since they could never understand them. Yet at times Campana was very amiable, generous, and in fact, a very timid soul. During all this period of fluctuating mental health he frequently gave vent to a refined lyrical taste.

Once more Campana was to leave Florence to wander into Switzerland. Later he is discovered in Turin trying to eke out a living by selling newspapers. In letters to his friends, he informed them of the love affair he was having with an Italian authoress. The poor girl however paid dearly for her affection. She was often beaten by him on the least provocation. It is no wonder that he was put in prison. From his cell he sent more letters to his friends, this time imploring them for financial assistance. The mental disease from which he was suffering was growing worse. He was finally confined to the Insane Asylum at Castel Pucci.

When we last were in Florence we drove by Castel Pucci with Carlo Carrà and Ardengo Soffici. Carrà expressed a desire to pay a visit to Campana but Soffici thought the visit might evoke tragic memories. So they decided not to go. Shortly thereafter we learned of Campana's death. While in the Asylum, Campana is said to have written some poems remarkable for their spontaneous expression of artistic images. Although friends have attempted to secure the originals of these lyrical compositions the hospital authorities have so far refused, claiming that they were being withheld because of their vital importance in the study of this unusually gifted but eccentric personality.

Dino Campana has tasted every form of human bitterness and enjoyed every degree of human exaltation, and he expresses his many varied and contrasting experiences of life in his poetry. In *Canti Orfici* there is a very deep and vibrant note of lyricism. There is a subtlety of taste and feeling in the "fragments" of the *Canti* that is rare. His was a life as rich spiritually as it was hard and bitter in material and physical comfort. But the personality that was Dino Campana will live for a long, long time in *Canti Orfici*. As is tragically inevitable in such cases, Italians are only now beginning to realize his worth and to pay homage to his art. In conclusion we should like to quote an estimate of Campana by his intimate friend, Bino Binazzi, who curiously enough, has also just passed away after a life almost as bitter and tragic. Of Campana, Binazzi wrote:

"Nella sua opera si sente la vibrazione lirica dell'anima del nostro popolo migrante in cerca di pane e di fortuna."

The following short extracts are representations of the poetic mood:

LA PETITE PROMENADE DU POETE

Me ne vado per le strade
Strette oscure e misteriose:
Vedo dietro le vetrate
Affacciarsi Gemme e Rose.
Dalle scale misteriose
C'è chi scende brancolando:
Dentro i vetri rilucenti
Stan le ciane commentando.

La stradina è solitaria:
Non c'è un cane: qualche stella
Nella notte sopra i tetti:
E la notte mi par bella.
E cammino poveretto
Nella notte fantasiosa,
Pur mi sento nella bocca.
La saliva disgustosa. Via dal tanfo
Via dal tanfo e per le strade
E cammina e via cammina,
Già le case son più rade.
Trovo l'erba; mi ci stendo
A conciarmi come un cane:
Da lontano un ubriaco
Canta amore alle persiane.

(Canti Orfici)

TOSCANA

L'Arno qui ancora ha tremiti freschi; poi lo occupa un silenzio dei più profondi: nel canale delle colline basse e monotone toccando le piccole città etrusche, uguale oramai sino alle foci, lasciando i bianchi trofei di Pisa, il duomo prezioso traversato dalla trave colossale, che chiude nella sua nudità un così vasto soffio marino. A Signa nel ronzìo musicale e assonnante ricordo quel profondo silenzio: il silenzio di un'epoca sepolta, di una civiltà sepolta: e come una fanciulla etrusca possa rattristare il paesaggio . . .

(Canti Orfici).

XIII.

EMILIO CECCHI

Emilio Cecchi was born in Florence in 1894. From his early youth he was intensely interested in art and literary criticism. People first began to know Cecchi through his articles in reviews and newspapers. As a collaborator of the *Voce,* Cecchi gave stimulating interpretations not only of Italian poetry but of English poetry as well. Soon after the war there appeared a volume entitled *Pesci Rossi,* a collection of critical writings which gained for Cecchi the esteem of many readers because of the delicacy and originality of literary workmanship.

We have often been disappointed in Cecchi as a journalist. His articles in the *Corriere della Sera* are still saturated with a haze of impenetrable meaning. They lack the lucidity so characteristic of many of the other collaborators of the *Voce.* But although there is much that is not clear even in such volumes as *Pesci Rossi* and *Osteria del Cattivo Tempo,* one is almost immediately aware, in reading Cecchi, that he is manifestly struggling to interpret an author's artistic creation as clearly and as succinctly as possible. As a matter of fact the reader feels that Cecchi is not only

147

trying to express the substance of a writer's thought but to express more than the writer himself has expressed and to say it even better. His critical formula consists of a pruning, sifting, and polishing process. When he is successful, and this is not infrequent, Cecchi is able to produce a work of genuine artistic merit and real literary intuition.

In his own ingenuous way Cecchi will often come out with reminiscences of travels and readings, with rare quotations yielded up as it were by a shipwreck. Then you discover that the ship had long been sought after and that perhaps what seemed a chance meeting was premeditated in order to show off this or that other jewel of a phrase or anecdote, like a young man in love who paces up and down the street through which he knows the object of his love must pass and who has the air of one who just chanced to wander there led by good fortune.

To fully understand the intellectual make-up and artistic idiosyncracies of Cecchi, however, one ought really to experience the pleasure of a personal acquaintanceship with him. Cecchi is at his best when he engages in conversation with you at his home or with his friends at the Caffè Aragno in Rome. Then he is more likely to give vent to his piquant irony and subtle sarcasm. It is an irony composed of the most varied artistic coloring. It is sharpened by the keenest and widest of literary and human experience. There are times when Cecchi's superior sensitiveness as critic and observer play havoc with our most traditionally established rules of logic and literary reasoning.

That is perhaps why Pancrazi, in his chapter on Cecchi in *Ragguagli di Parnaso,* believes that it is easier to be struck by an analysis than by a judgment of Cecchi. And our own experience tempts us to agree with Pancrazi.

Emilio Cecchi, versatile writer of poems, essays, travels, and histories of art and literature, has made not a few critical excursions into the field of English and American letters, a work on Rudyard Kipling having appeared in 1911 and the first volume of a *Storia della letteratura inglese nel secolo XIX* in 1915. His recent book entitled *Scrittori inglesi e americani* (Milano, Carabba, 1935) consists of a series of sketches, anecdotal, biographical and critical, on English and American writers from Byron to Virginia Woolf, including Carlyle, Melville, Poe, Tennyson, Swinburne, Pater, O. Henry, Faulkner, and many others. Each essay, no matter how slight in size, tends to be broad in scope and to drive toward a point or general idea, often luminously established. In each, though in some more than in others, literary gossip is worked up to a pitch where it reveals genuine ideas about life and art and their subtle relationships. Taken as a whole, they offer us a fascinating glimpse into the workshop of a bona fide critic's, not a book-reviewer's, mind.

The publication of Cecchi's recent books *Qualche Cosa,* and *Messico,* has brought up again the question of the relative merits of the Italian writers of a generation ago and the merits of those who have won their literary spurs during the past few years. Sergio Solmi, writing about Cecchi in

L'Italia Letteraria of April 10, 1932, said that he was very curious to know how much the younger generation of Italian writers owes to Cecchi in the way of ideas and in the way of method; and by method he meant specifically *metodo vivo nel considerare gli uomini e le opere, non dell'astratto metodo dei teorici.*

Sitting with a group of young writers at a café in Florence, not so long ago, we listened attentively to a bitter denunciation of the older generation of Italian writers. The young author who was doing the talking seemed to be thoroughly convinced that the *Vociani* or collaborators of the *Voce,* had become just so many literary cobwebs of antiquity. And by *Vociani* our excited critic obviously meant Prezzolini, Papini, Soffici, Croce, Gentile, and last but not least Cecchi. Even the most disinterested listener could not help but feel, however, that the flatulent and frothy language of the young speaker betrayed unsound reasoning and prejudice in his argument.

In order to avoid the errors and pitfalls of the *Vociani* many young Italians have been blinded to the excellent literary qualities of the *Voce* writers. Any present day writer would do well to study, analyze, and emulate them. The greatest handicap the young author in Italy has to meet today is the lack of a thorough appreciation of the literary experiences of his immediate or even remote predecessors. If one were to take the works of a representative of the new school of Italian authors and to compare them with those of any of the *Voce* collaborators there would be little doubt, even in the mind of the most enthusiastic spokesman of the younger group, that the latter has still a long way to go to catch up with the literary technique and wide experience of an Emilio Cecchi.

XIV.

FRANCESCO LANZA

The death, recently, of Francesco Lanza at the age of thirty-five has deprived Italy of one of its most promising writers. Lanza, who incidentally was a Sicilian by birth, was no ordinary man-of-letters. He was the exponent of no new theory of art, nor was he the shadow of any favorite predecessor or contemporary. In these days of so much literary astigmatism Francesco Lanza had the good fortune of being endowed with an unusually fine literary vision. He was one of those who could see life with his own naked eye.

Lanza in his *Mimi Siciliani* (Milano, Alpes, 1928) has produced one of the most outstanding literary productions of the past decade. In this work one finds a clarity and succinctness of images and a freshness and originality of narrative expression that are particularly exhilarating for one accustomed to a literary atmosphere heavy with the mist of obfuscated theories of art and style. These short snapshots of Sicilian life portray the naiveté and customs of a peasant people with a delicacy of humor and a subtlety of satire to delight the taste of the most exacting reader of present-day Italian letters. What is especially attractive in Lanza is that he tells his stories without the superfluous literary trimmings prevalent in the works of many Italian *letterati*. In the *Mimi* you feel the author has been preoccupied more with pruning and cutting than with decorating and adding. There seems to be a conscious dislike for any ornamentation. Lanza's literary products are as indigenous, as natural, and as rugged as the Sicilian countryside itself. Brevity and conciseness of expression add to rather than detract from what the author wishes to say. Rich and sharply defined pictures are given in few words, in short but poignant phrases. Lanza thus provides literary nourishment of the most concentrated form.

In life as in letters Lanza was esteemed by all who had the privilege to know him, for he always tried to be himself, as natural in his personal dealings as he was in his literary endeavors. Upon leaving Sicily some years ago he came to Rome to establish himself as a journalist. Credit for his discovery must be given to Lombardo-Radice who first saw in him a writer of unusual merit. We first met Lanza at the Caffè Aragno chatting with his friends Cecchi, Cardarelli, Ungaretti, Alvaro. The first thing that impressed us was the simplicity of his dress, and the reticence and modesty of his speech. He was extremely timid and shy as a country boy.

As a matter of fact, we learned that he was always obsessed with the fear that he was writing stuff that had little, if any, literary merit. He had often wished to veil his identity, requesting that his articles appear anonymously. It was only when Mussolini, after his trip to

Grosseto, revealed that he liked Lanza's best of all the published reports of his journey, that our young writer took courage and decided to carry on. A few months before his death appeared Lanza's last volume entitled, *All'albergo del Sole*, Firenze, Solaria, 1932. In it Lanza gives evidence of the same concentration of thought and the same depth of feeling that characterize all his works. The following morsel from *Mimi Siciliani* is a modest sample of the treat that is in store for readers of that beloved personality that was once Francesco Lanza:

LA LUNA ED IL PIAZZESE

Due mazzarinesi, 'imbriachi fino alle nasche come scimmie, uscirono dalla taverna ch'era notte; e per ragionarla meglio se n'andavano a braccetto a piacere dei piedi, un passo avanti e due indietro, che parevano a mare.

A un punto, sul campanile della chiesa si levò la luna, tonda come una ruota e tutta raggiante; e quelli, che gli pesava il vino, restarono alluciati a mirarla.

Uno della partita, ch'era il più colto, gli parve il sole e mostrandola al compagno faceva:

— Guardate, compare mio, che ci è spuntato il sole tra' piedi, noi non ce ne siamo accorti.

E l'altro, per non dargliela vinta:

— Gnornò che non è il sole, ma la luna, che i galli non cantano.

E quello:

— E io vi dico che è il sole.

— E io, che è la luna.

E il sole è la luna, nessuno se la voleva dar persa, e se non era che non stavano dritti finiva a zuffa. Finalmente, si trovava a passare di là il piazzese, che iva a Mazzarino pei fatti suoi; e quelli vedendolo si volsero a lui, che dicesse la sua:

— O voi messere, è quello il sole, o la luna?

E il piazzese:

— Abbò, io forestiero sono!

XV.

EUGENIO MONTALE

When you enter the spacious reading room of the Vieusseux Library of Florence and proceed to walk past the book racks to the far corner on the left, you will find yourself on the threshold of the office of Eugenio Montale, director of the Gabinetto Vieusseux in Palazzo di Parte Guelfa.

A peep through the window pane of the door leading to the office assures you that the director cannot be in, for there is only a young man standing at a counter in the dark room, very likely engaged in cutting the leaves of a review or skimming through the pages of a new book. Surely the director of the Vieusseux Library must be an elderly man, carelessly dressed, with stooped shoulders, and white beard. But upon inquiry the well-groomed young man of thirty odd years startles you with the information that "the director is in" and that he himself is Eugenio Montale. And your preconceived notions about the physical appearance of the director are rudely upset. But not any more so than any preconceived notions you may entertain concerning the poetry of Eugenio Montale.

Montale published several years ago a volume of verse entitled *Ossi di Seppia.* In the judgment of certain discriminating lovers of poetry who bothered to read that volume when it first appeared there seemed to be no doubt that it represented a milestone in the development of contemporary Italian poetry. One day we inquired of our esteemed friend, Aldo Palazzeschi, what he thought of Montale as a poet. When Palazzeschi informed us that, in his opinion, Montale was perhaps the only outstanding poet of the younger generation in Italy we immediately set out to purchase a copy of *Ossi di Seppia*. We tried several booksellers without success. The first edition of several hundred copies was out of print. We learned that there had been a second edition and that it too had been exhausted. The more we inquired about a copy of *Ossi di Seppia* the more interesting was the data we gathered concerning the author. Finally our appetite became so whetted we determined to go directly to Montale. We pleaded so well that he offered us one of the two remaining copies in his posssession. Having met Montale the library director, we sat down that evening to become acquainted with Montale the poet.

We confess that our first reading of *Ossi di Seppia* did not impress us very much. Or rather we should say we were impressed—but more by the difficulty of trying to understand the author than by any beauty of form or expression. Since then, however, we have had occasion to reread the volume and we have taken the necessary leisure to study and compare it with a number of contemporary volumes of verse. The poetry of Montale is not the usual effusion of lyricism that comes out from the fount of Italian traditionalism. There is little if any of the *letterato* in him. The inspiration for his lyre he seeks not in the experiences of other poets nor in those of any school of poetry. All he does is to go into his own back-yard of experiences, tap the sources of his own environment, and colorful, spontaneous and original poetic images gush forth!

The experiences of Montale are not provincial or local in character. He has a message to transmit that has an appeal for those who live beyond the confines of his native country. In *Ossi di Seppia* we are confronted with the unsolved tragedy of a spiritually shipwrecked individual who has lost his bearings in the unfathomable enigma of life. *Se un'ombra scorgete non è un'ombra, ma quella io sono.* (If you perceive a shadow, it is not a shadow, it is I.).

In his repeated wanderings along the shores of this terrestrial life Montale is constantly stubbing his toes against sharp stones or cutting his feet on blade-like shells or glittering glass. "Poesia pietrosa" someone has aptly termed it. As Consiglio observes, Montale finds himself buried between the mausoleums of two faiths: that of the past and that of the future. Yet he never ceases to look about for a new one even though he finds himself surrounded by a wall "che ha cocci aguzzi di bottiglia". What is remarkable in Montale is that he is never overcome by the futility of it all "animi arsi in cui l'illusione brucia un fuoco pieno di cenere". The futility of existence is conquered by a recognized and acknowledged non-existence. This poet is constantly conscious of a life he hasn't lived and yet cannot help but feel. He is forever seeking the "the vita non vissuta". There seems to be a constant struggle between disintegrating matter on the one hand and an immanent aspiration to seek a synthetic form on the other. The effect on the reader is most unusual. Amidst this "impietrato soffrire senza nome", amidst this critical corrosion of existence, amidst this desert waste of rugged stones, sharp pebbles, and broken glass, the poetry of Montale is like a refreshing stream of clear water—"un'acqua limpida scorta per avventura tra le petraie d'un greto."

It is not to be wondered then, that Montale has attracted the attention of discerning readers in Italy. Nor is it to be wondered that he is esteemed by T. S. Eliot who recently saw fit to publish translations of his verse in the Criterion— a rare honor for an Italian poet of today.

XVI.

ALBERTO MORAVIA

Alberto Moravia was born in Rome, November 29, 1907, of a Venetian father who is now an architect in Rome, and of a mother who originally came from Le Marche. Young Alberto never attended school but was educated at home and is practically self-taught and self-educated. At the age of eleven he began to write poems in French and Italian. The French compositions were inspired by Baudelaire while those in Italian were inspired by Carducci and D'Annunzio. At fourteen this precocious young man wrote his first novel and before reaching the age of seventeen he had already completed four novels, all of which, he says: "I fortunately burned".

Then for three years he devoted himself to the writing of *Gli Indifferenti*, finishing it when he was twenty but after having re-written it three times. Upon the completion of the manuscript Moravia went in high hopes to an Italian publisher but the manuscript was rejected. He tried several others but they too refused it with the general criticism that it was a hodge-podge of words —one of them described the work as a "nebbia di parole". Finally Moravia had to advance the money for publication to the firm of Alpes of Milan.

We chanced to be in Italy in 1929 when the book made its appearance and we recall very well how it was first hailed by the critic, G. A. Borgese in the columns of the *Corriere della Sera*. Almost overnight Moravia's name was on the lip of every important man-of-letters in Italy. Four editions of the novel were printed in the space of one year—a remarkable achievement for a contemporary Italian author.

At first the novel found its readers divided in their estimate of the author. There were those who praised Moravia very warmly for his unusual success while others were just as strong in their condemnation of the pessimism of the author and more particularly of his portrayal of the Italian family whose life he so vividly describes in the book. There was a general concurrence of opinion, however, as to the unmistakable inherent literary qualities of the young author. At all events *Gli Indifferenti* became the favorite subject of discussion in many literary cafés of Italy. Translations of the novel appeared in English, in French, in Czecho-Slovak, in Hungarian, in Dutch and even in Danish.

Some critics of Moravia made the mistake of concluding that since the book describes so vividly the complete moral corruption and human disintegration of each member of a deplorable and spineless family, bound only by ties of self-interest and indifference, the novel is immoral and its author a depraved and pessimistic individual. On the contrary, if one stops to consider the novel objectively one cannot help but see, through the apparent maze of immorality and pessimism, the author's inherent craving for a more human and brighter concept of life. To give a clear, minute and analytical description of vanishing moral values does not necessarily mean to approve depravity nor even to preach pessimism. Moravia considers himself a realist, in the sense that realism implies an objective attitude that is devoid of any passion. Anyone who has had the opportunity to know Moravia cannot fail to discern in his apparently cynical outlook on life an innate craving for optimism and a truly moral existence.

Since the publication of *Gli Indifferenti* Moravia has contributed to *La Stampa* of Turin. During his recent sojourn in England he was the correspondent of *La Gazzetta del Popolo,* also of Turin. In recent years Moravia has published *La Bella Vita* (Carabba 1935), *L'Ambizione Sbagliata* (Mondadori 1935) and *L'Imbroglio* (Bompiani 1937), but none of these works has so far created any stir comparable to *Gli Indifferenti,* although some critics have noted in them unmistakable progress in style.

La Bella Vita and *L'Imbroglio* contain short stories in which Moravia develops "a treatise on human cruelty." He dissects with rare skill the cruelest, meanest, and most wretched of souls, yet Moravia makes the motives of their human behavior sound very plausible.

The Viking Press of New York recently published Alberto Moravia's novel *L'Ambizione sbagliata* under the English title of the *Wheel of Fortune.* The excellent translation is the work of Arthur Livingston. To try to link the characters of this book to a Fascist Italy (as some critics have done) is only more ridiculous than confining them to Italy at all — or to any one country. A group of such depraved malicious and evil people as one meets in *Wheel of Fortune* might be found not only in Rome but in any large city of the world. Perhaps it might not be possible elsewhere, however, to find a writer like Moravia, capable of describing such a society. It has been amusing to notice the early critical reactions of this book in the American press. Critics wondered why a reader should want to remember the tragic figure of Andreina or the cripple Stefano, mean, cruel and rotten. These critics fail to realize that a painter may depict a very revolting scene on a canvas and yet the artistic results attained may be most beautiful.

Viewed in this light we cannot help but feel that *Wheel of Fortune* should serve as a great moral stimulus rather than a "horrifying picture of the decadence and greed of a certain segment of Italian society" as one American critic termed it.

We had the pleasure of becoming acquainted with Moravia in Rome a few months after the appearance of his first novel and we remember to this day how we marveled at his extensive learning. He was among the very few of the many Italian authors we met who had a knowledge of contemporary American literature. Moravia's favorite American authors are Hemingway, Faulkner, Dos Passos and Sherwood Anderson. He has translated some of De Foe and Hem-

ingway into Italian.   He says he doesn't like
Dreiser because he finds his style much too heavy
and journalistic. Other American authors whom
he has admired are Poe, Hawthorne and Herman
Melville. His favorite contemporary Italian writers are Palazzeschi, Croce, Ungaretti, the early
Soffici, Baldini and Malaparte.

Of interest to Americans may be Moravia's
attempt to define and analyze that illusive animal,
homo americanus. What struck Moravia full in
the face during his recent visit to America was the
lack of homogeneity in the character of the American. He finds here an eclectic mixture of many
cultures devoid of any connecting ingredients.
He attributes this to the fact that emigrants dropped all their previous ties and adjusted themselves
to their new environment on its lowest level—the
economic. Then, when *homo americanus* realizes
that he is only one of millions in the tremendous
urban centers, he often goes about satisfying his
desire hedonistically, paying slight attention to
spiritual values. For this reason Americans have
no set ideas, the ones they do have are acquired
ready-made—hence their slight critical sense which
makes them condone almost anything. What
leaves Moravia disconcerted is the perfect harmony
with which this civilization functions and the
realization that the tendencies now prevalent in
Europe tend to bring about this state of affairs.

It may be interesting to note here Moravia's
views on the European novel in the nineteenth
century. According to Moravia, the nineteenth
century represents the decadence or better the distortion of the novel. This very great and hybrid

165

century started auspiciously but ended badly. It began with the exemplary biographies of Constant, Dickens, Thackery, Stendhal, Balzac, and concluded with the stupidities and nonsense of the historical novel and with the old rubbish and census-taking of the naturalists. One may already detect this decadence in the minutely and not always necessary descriptions of Balzac, Walter Scott and Hugo. It was left to the more primitive Russians to restore the great tradition of the novel. Joyce instead, and even more Proust belong outright to the nineteenth century. The trifles, the confusion, the fragmentariness, all the disorder and incongruities of that century reach their culmination and apotheosis with these two authors. There is more feeling for the novel in a yellow book than in all Proust. Moravia believes that after these two experiences the sense of human biography will certainly be reborn and in so rigorous and succinct a manner, and through ways so unexpected, that it will seem like the greatest of innovations.

XVII.

CORRADO ALVARO

Gente in Aspromonte by Corrado Alvaro had the distinction recently of carrying off the coveted prize of 50,000 lire offered by *La Stampa* of Turin for the best novel of the year published in Italy. That this book of Corrado Alvaro is worthy of such recognition is not difficult to understand if we pause a moment to consider the work of this young writer who hails from Calabria and spends most of his time in Rome trying to eke out a living by the use of his pen.

Alvaro first caught the public eye by a series of short stories that contained interesting cross-sections of the primitive and rustic life of his native Calabria. In *L'Amata alla Finestra,* an earlier work, and in the prize volume *Gente in Aspromonte,* Alvaro offers a collection of Calabrian scenes colored with the sharp tints of an intense realism and of a deep melancholy which make the reading of them a delightful treat, especially if one compares these writings of Alvaro with those of the vast majority of his literary contemporaries. Furthermore, a perusal of Alvaro's work reveals a literary technique that is devoid of the superfluously decorative flourishes that have been the curse of so many Italian writers. The

167

sharp, barren and rugged coast of Calabria and the hard, primitive and passionate life of the people are depicted in a style that enhances the beauty and charm of the literary pictures. And with what depth and effect does the pen of Alvaro dip into the very heart and soul of the Calabrian country-side and the Calabrian family life! The reader cannot help but feel an obvious subsequent effect on his own spiritual vision.

There are authors who write novels that are nothing more nor less than descriptions of the region or environment from which they have sprung. These are sometimes called regional-ists and as such their work often appeals only to a limited few. On the other hand there are writers who use the region or environment in which they live to reveal and give expression to their own soul. These have naturally a more universal ap-peal and have something more substantial to offer in the way of spiritually stimulating substance. And Corrado Alvaro is among those who belong to this second category.

In *Gente in Aspromonte*, Alvaro does not describe Calabria so much as he describes himself —a humble, melancholy and extremely sensitive being, moulded by the poverty, the hardships and disappointments of life. When Alvaro takes us on his excursions through Calabria we find our guide equipped with an especially fine pair of spiritual field glasses. And it is with these field glasses that Alvaro makes us scan the horizon of life—a horizon saturated with a grey mist but whose outline is sufficiently distinguished by the few penetrating rays of sunlight.

There is in the work of Alvaro a good deal that is reminiscent of the atmosphere and thought of such writers as Proust and Freud. This may readily be noted in the passions, the sex problems, the emotional struggles of his characters who try to adapt themselves to a life and environment dominated by the power of the senses, the sentiment, the sensual.

We had the pleasure of making the personal acquaintance of Alvaro in Rome at a café. We shall never forget how disappointed we were when we first met him. The expectations and the actualities were so different. We imagined a tall, middleaged individual with sharply intelligent features and a hardened expression of life on his countenance. Instead, we met a short stocky young man, very humble and modest in appearance and with an almost naïve expression on his face. We had just returned from a trip through Calabria and had expected to find a more representative physical exponent of the region.

Alvaro is very anxious to come to America to train his appraising eye on the *panorama* of American life, not so much with the intention of reproducing what he will see into literary form as with a view toward taking in new scenes and strengthening his own vision of life.

XVIII.

DELFINO CINELLI

Not more than a few years ago, Delfino Cinelli was absolutely unknown in Italy as a writer. At that time the Cinellis of Florence were known as hat manufacturers and the young Cinelli was busy helping his father to export hats to all parts of the world. Then suddenly, in 1928, there appeared in the bookshops of Italy two novels, one entitled *Castiglion che Dio sol sa* and the other, *La Trappola* and in a few weeks the name of Cinelli was to be conjured with not only in commercial but in literary circles as well.

A few months after the publication of *Castiglion che Dio sol sa* we happened to be in Italy on a literary mission. The great stir created by Cinelli's novel and the fact that a Florentine merchant had turned author—a rare event in the annals of Italian literature—aroused our curiosity. We decided to look up Cinelli and in true journalistic fashion we set out for a lead.

We scoured the literary cafés of Florence but discovered that he was not among the frequenters. Apparently he did not belong to any particular clique and his name was found missing among the representatives of the various opposing schools of literary thought. We should have made inquiries at the hat stores but at the time we did not know that Cinelli had served his literary apprenticeship as a Florentine merchant. At last we obtained a clue. One day we were informed that Cinelli was supposed to be a good friend of the "enfant terrible" of Italian literature — Giovanni Papini.

Hot on the trail we betook ourselves to Papini's house. There we sadly learned that Cinelli was out of town. Before leaving, however, we obtained from Papini more data concerning our mysterious author. Among other things Papini declared that, in his opinion, Cinelli was one of the two most promising writers of the day in Italy. He urged us to be sure to make his acquaintance. This comment by Papini served to whet our appetite all the more. Then we learned that Cinelli had been awarded the much coveted Mondadori prize for the best novel of the year — especially significant since the book was not a Mondadori publication. We determined to pursue by all means the hunt for this unusual and elusive author. Unfortunately, however, every time we made new inquiries Cinelli was not to be found. After several months we were obliged to leave Florence without having succeeded in getting even a glimpse of him.

One may imagine our surprise therefore, when, one bright day, whom should we run into on the campus of Columbia University but Cinelli himself! "Caught at last!" we shouted in exultation to ourselves. We proceeded immediately to make him our prisoner and in no time sentenced him to a luncheon engagement at the Faculty Club.

172

Once at the Club we lost no time in proceding to make our guest submit to a long and belated cross-examination concerning his past and his future. At first reticent and reluctant to speak either about himself or his work, he finally succumbed to the constant bombardment of questions. The following is the cross-examination which we reproduce to the best of our recollection:

"When and where were you born?"

"At Siena in 1889."

"What schooling have you had?"

"The usual elementary education. For a while I attended a *collegio* at Prato."

"Then what happened?"

"Well,—" and here there was a long disconcerting pause, "then I traveled for study in Switzerland and England. Later I joined my father in his hat business and I began to make frequent trips to the United States and Porto Rico. I was twenty-one when I first came to New York to open an office for my father."

"How often have you been to the United States?"

"Oh, very often. I guess I have crossed the Atlantic some fifty times. You know I'm married to an American girl."

"No, really?"

"Why yes, and she and I translated *La Trappola* (The Trap) published recently by John Day & Company."

"But during the time you were busy with your father did you ever manifest any literary proclivities?"

"I used to like to read and was always a

173

great admirer of Tozzi and of Verga. Occasionally I wrote a verse or two and one day I published a little volume of poetry which had a moderate success."

"Well, how did you come to write *Castiglion che Dio sol sa?*"

"A few years ago I decided not to devote so much time to my father's business but to spend more time on the family estate in the Maremma. I felt a craving for the soil and an ardent desire to give literary expression to my love for that deserted, marshy and austere region that is peopled by patient, hard working and sturdy peasants."

"From what I gather then, the power of the redemption of the soil, (*la redenzione della terra*) and the characterization of a rustic people —*rinselvaggito*—are the two pillars on which the structure of *Castiglion che Dio sol sa* is built."

"I imagine so."

"And what about your other books, *La Trappola, Calafùria, Cinque Mila Lire,* and *La Carriera di Riccardo Bonòmini,* etc.?"

"*The Trap* or *La Trappola* is a rustic tragedy. *Calafùria* depicts love's struggle against inevitable circumstances. It is a melodramatic *romanzo vecchio tipo* while *Riccardo Bonòmini* is a character study."

"Which of these books has had the greatest success?"

"*The Trap*, but personally I like *Castiglion* the best of the novels I've written."

"Besides writing for *Pègaso, La Nuova An-*

tologia and other reviews are you doing any other literary work these days?"

"Why let me see. Yes, my next novel will be the story of an Italo-American and the title will be *Lucia*. I have already sent in the first installment to *Pègaso* and it will first appear serially in that review."

At this juncture we looked at the Faculty Club clock and noticed it was time for class. With much reluctance we took our leave of Cinelli. That evening at home, we reread "The Trap" and found it a very ingenious tale. Cinelli paints his background with simple but poignant phrases. He is particularly successful when he depicts the rustic austere life of the Maremma and the clash of the strong and impulsive passions of its people. In Cinelli, there is more life than literature. The reader is more likely to be impressed by what the author has to say than by the way he says it. He knows the common people, understands their life, their emotions, their joys their sorrows.

Cinelli speaks of "the merciful qualities of memory which, with the passing of time, seem not only to diminish and forgive the bitterness and rancor of the past but may even make sorrows eventually assume a beautiful aspect through recollection."

With this thought in mind, we conclude our consideration of Cinelli and of contemporary Italian letters in general.

175

A SELECTED BIBLIOGRAPHY OF CONTEMPORARY ITALIAN LITERATURE

The following bibliography contains a list of important Italian books published since 1900. Obviously the list gives expression to our own individual taste. There are changes and substitutions in titles and authors that might readily be made to suit particular needs or other individual tastes. The list does not pretend to be authoritive or final. Its primary aim is to meet the needs and interests of the average reader in this country who might find it useful as a point of departure in the study of current letters and thought in Italy.

GENERAL REFERENCE WORKS

(Anthologies, Critical and Philosophical Studies, Histories, etc.)

Borgese, G. A.	*La vita e il libro.* Tre serie. Bocca, Torino.
Crémieux, B.	*Panorame de la litterature italienne contemporaine.* Paris, Kra.
Chi è?	*Dizionario degli Italiani d'Oggi.* Formiggini, Roma.
Croce, B.	*La Letteratura della Nuova Italia.* Bari, Laterza.
	Estetica. Bari, Laterza.
	Storia d'Italia. Bari, Laterza.
D'Amico, Silvio	*Il Teatro Italiano.* Milano, Treves.
Falqui e Vittorini	*Scrittori nuovi (Antologia Italiana*
Flora, Francesco	*Contemporanea)* Lanciano, Carabba.
	Dal Romanticismo al Futurismo. Milano, Mondadori.
Gentile, Giovanni	*Che cosa è il fascismo.* Firenze, Vallecchi.
	Sommario di pedagogia come scienza filosofica. Bari, Laterza.

Giacobbe, Olinto	*Le più belle pagine dei poeti d'oggi.* Antologia, Lanciano, Carabba.
Lombardo-Radice, G.	*Lezioni di didattica.* Palermo, Sandron.
Missiroli, Mario	*L'Italia d'Oggi.* Bologna, Zanichelli.
Momigliano, A.	*Impressioni di un lettore contemporaneo.* Mondadori, Milano.
Pancrazi, P.	*Venti uomini, un satiro e un burattino.* Firenze, Vallecchi.
	Scrittori italiani del novecento. Bari, Laterza.
Panzini, Alfredo	*Dizionario moderno.* Milano, Hoepli.
Papini e Pancrazi	*Poeti d'oggi* (1900-25). Firenze, Vallecchi.
Papini, Giovanni	*Stroncature.* Firenze, Vallecchi.
Pellizzi, C.	*Lettere italiane del nostro secolo.* Milano, Libreria d'Italia.
Prezzolini, G.	*La Cultura italiana.* Milano, Edizioni Corbaccio.
Ravegnani, Giuseppe	*I Contemporanei.* Torino, Bocca.
Russo, L.	*I narratori, guida bibliografica.* Leonardo, Roma.
Sarfatti, Margherita	*Dux.* Milano, Mondadori.
Serra, R.	*Le lettere,* 2 vol. Firenze, La Voce.
	Saggi critici. La Voce, Roma.
Soffici, Ardengo	*Scoperte e Massacri.* Vallecchi, Firenze.
Thovez, E.	*Il pastore, il gregge, e la zampogna.* Ricciardi, Napoli.
Tilgher, Adriano	*Voci del tempo.* Libreria di Scienze e lettere. Roma.
Titta Rosa, G.	*Narratori contemporanei.* 2 vol. Il Primato, Milano.
Volpe, G.	*L'Italia in cammino.* Milano, Treves.

NOVELS, SHORT STORIES, ESSAYS, ETC.

Aleramo, Sibilla	*Una donna.* Firenze, Bemporad.
Alvaro, Corrado	*Gente in Aspromonte.* Treves, Milano.
Bacchelli, Riccardo	*Il Diavolo al Pontelungo.* Ceschina Milano.
Baldini, Antonio	*Michelaccio.* La Ronda editrice, Roma.
Barilli, Bruno	*Il Paese del Melodramma.* Carabba,

Bartolini, Luigi	*Passeggiata con la ragazza*. Firenze, Vallecchi.
Beltramelli, Antonio	*Il Cav. Mostardo*. Milano, Mondadori. *Gli uomini rossi*.
Bontempelli, Massimo	*Il figlio di due madri*. Roma, Edizioni "900".
Borgese, Giuseppe A.	*Rubè*. Milano, Treves.
Cardarelli, Vincenzo	*Parliamo dell'Italia*. Firenze, Vallecchi.
Cecchi, Emilio	*Messico*. Milano, Treves. *Qualche cosa*. Lanciano, Carabba.
Chiesa, Francesco	*Istorie e favole*. Genova, Formiggini. *Racconti puerili*. Roma, Formiggini.
Cicognani, Bruno	*Villa Beatrice*. Milano, Treves.
Cinelli, Delfino	*Castiglion che Dio sol sa*. Milano, "L'Eroica".
D'Annunzio, G.	*Notturno*. Milano, Treves.
Deledda, Grazia	*Il vecchio della montagna*. Milano, Treves.
Fogazzaro, Antonio	*Il Santo*. Milano, Baldini.
Fracchia, Umberto	*La Stella del nord*. Mondadori, Milano.
Gadda, Piero	*Mozzo*. Milano, Ceschina.
Jahier, Piero	*Con me e con gli alpini*. Roma, La Voce.
Lanza, Francesco	*Mimi Siciliani*. Milano, Alpes.
Loria, Arturo	*La Scuola di Ballo*. Firenze, Edizione di Solaria.
Malaparte, Curzio (Suckert)	*Italia Barbara*. La Voce, Roma. *Le avventure di un capitano di sventura*. Bologna, La Voce.
Martini, Fausto Maria	*Si sbarca a Nuova York*. 1931. Verona, Mondadori.
Masino, Paola	*Periferia*, Bompiani.
Moravia, Alberto	*Gli indifferenti*. Alpes, Milano.
Negri, Ada	*Stella Mattutina*. Mondadori, Milano.
Ojetti, U.	*Cose Viste*. Milano, Treves.
Palazzeschi, Aldo	*Stampe dell'Ottocento*. Milano, Treves.
Panzini, Alfredo	*La Lanterna di Diogene*. Treves, Milano. *Il viaggio di un povero letterato*. Treves, Milano. *Santippe*. Treves, Milano.

Papini, Giovanni	*Un uomo finito.* Vallecchi, Firenze.
	Storia di Cristo. Vallecchi, Firenze.
	Gog. Vallecchi, Firenze.
Pea, Enrico	*Moscardino.* Treves, Milano.
Pirandello, Luigi	*Novelle.* Firenze, Bemporad.
	Il fu Mattia Pascal. Firenze, Bemporad.
Provenzal, Dino	*Le passeggiate di Bardalone.*
San Secondo, Rosso di	*La Fuga.*
Slataper, Scipio	*Il mio Carso.* Roma, La Voce.
Soffici, Ardengo	*Arlecchino.* Vallecchi, Firenze.
	Giornale di Bordo. Vallecchi, Firenze.
Svevo, Italo	*La coscienza di Zeno.* Cappelli, Bologna.
Tecchi, Bonaventura	*Il vento tra le case.* Torino, Ribet.
Tozzi, Federico	*Tre croci.* Milano, Treves.
Vivanti, Annie	*I divoratori.* Milano, Treves.

POETRY

Corazzini, Sergio	*Liriche.* Napoli, Ricciardi.
Di Giacomo, Salvatore	*Poesie.* Napoli, Ricciardi.
Govoni, Corrado	*Poesie Scelte.* Ferrara, Taddei.
Gozzano, Guido	*La via del rifugio.* Torino, Streglio.
Montale, Eugenio	*Ossi di Seppia.* Torino, Ribet.
Moretti, Marino	*Poesie (1905-14).* Milano, Treves.
Novaro, Angiolo S.	*Il Cestello (Poesie per i piccoli).* Milano, Treves, 1920.
Palazzeschi, Aldo	*Poesie.* (1904-1909) Firenze, Vallecchi.
Papini, Giovanni	*Cento pagine di poesia.* Vallecchi, Firenze.
Saba, Umberto	*Canzoniere* (tutta l'opera poetica fino al 1921). Milano, Treves.
Trilussa	*Giove e le bestie.* Mondadori, Milano.
Ungaretti, Giuseppe	*Allegria di naufragi.* Vallecchi, Firenze.
Valeri, Diego	*Poesie.*

THEATRE

Benelli, S.	*Tignola.* 1908.
	La cena delle beffe. Milano, Treves, 1925.
Bracco, R.	*Sperduti nel buio.*
	La piccola fonte. Milano, Sandron.
Campanile, A.	*L'amore fa fare questo e altro.*
Chiarelli, L.	*La maschera e il volto.* **Milano,** Treves.
Corradini, E.	*Giulio Cesare.*
D'Annunzio, G.	*La figlia di Iorio.* Milano, Treves.
De Stefani, A.	*Il calzolaio di Messina.*
Giacosa, G.	*Come le foglie.* Milano, Treves.
Marinetti, F.	*Re Baldoria.* Milano, Treves.
Martini, F. M.	*Il fiore sotto gli occhi.* Milano, Mondadori.
Morselli, E. L.	*Orione.* Milano, Treves.
	Glauco. Milano, Treves.
Niccodemi, D.	*Scampolo.* Milano, Treves.
Oxilia e Camasio	*Addio giovinezza.* Ivrea, Viassone.
Pirandello, L.	*Lumie di Sicilia.* Firenze, Bemporad.
	Pensaci Giacomino. Firenze, Bemporad.
	Così è se vi pare. Firenze, Bemporad.
	Sei personaggi in cerca di autore.
	Enrico IV. Firenze, Bemporad.
San Secondo, Rosso di	*Marionette, che passione.*
Verga, G.	*Caccia al lupo.*

181

INDEX OF NAMES